The Discourse of Ethics and Equity in Intercultural Communication

This book examines the notions of ethics and equity in relation to language and communication in intercultural relations. Although these notions are often discussed, they are not always addressed with regard to specific subjects. Much intercultural discourse and dialogue in recent times has been coloured by the clash of civilizations (as described by Samuel Huntington), terrorist attacks such as 9/11, and the indelible effects which these events have had on dealings between different peoples, cultures and religions. This book discusses ethics and equity with regard to marginalized and privileged minorities, victims of abuse and of conflict, researchers and practitioners, and language learners and speaker/users. It opens up spaces for a critical discourse of ethics and equity in language and intercultural communication as 'new' knowledge.

This book was originally published as a special issue of *Language and Intercultural Communication*.

Shanta Nair-Venugopal is an Associate Fellow at the Institute of Malaysian and International Studies (IKMAS), National University of Malaysia/UKM where she was recently a guest scholar. She was previously Principal Fellow at the Institute of Occidental Studies, and prior to that Professor in the School of Language Studies and Linguistics, also at the National University of Malaysia/UKM. She has published internationally in the areas of language, discourse and intercultural communication in referred journals, books and other compilations. A more recent publication is *The Gaze of the West and Framings of the East* (Palgrave Macmillan, 2012).

The Discourse of Ethics and Equity in Intercultural Communication

Edited by
Shanta Nair-Venugopal

LONDON AND NEW YORK

First published 2016
by Routledge

2 Park Square, Milton Park, Abingdon, Oxon OX14 4RN
711 Third Avenue, New York, NY 10017, USA

Routledge is an imprint of the Taylor & Francis Group, an informa business

First issued in paperback 2017

British Library Cataloguing in Publication Data
A catalogue record for this book is available from the British Library

ISBN 13: 978-1-138-92412-3 (hbk)
ISBN 13: 978-1-138-09494-9 (pbk)

Typeset in Times
by RefineCatch Limited, Bungay, Suffolk

Publisher's Note
The publisher accepts responsibility for any inconsistencies that may have arisen during the conversion of this book from journal articles to book chapters, namely the possible inclusion of journal terminology.

Disclaimer
Every effort has been made to contact copyright holders for their permission to reprint material in this book. The publishers would be grateful to hear from any copyright holder who is not here acknowledged and will undertake to rectify any errors or omissions in future editions of this book.

Contents

Citation Information   vii

Notes on Contributors   ix

Introduction: the discourse of ethics and equity   1
Shanta Nair-Venugopal

1. Intercultural ethics: questions of methods in language
   and intercultural communication   10
   Alison Phipps

2. The uses of oral history in Cyprus: ethics, memory and identity   27
   Holger Briel

3. Beyond the reach of ethics and equity? Depersonalisation and
   dehumanisation in foreign domestic helper narratives   44
   Hans J. Ladegaard

4. Issues of language choice, ethics and equity: Japanese retirees
   living in Malaysia as their second home   60
   Siti Hamin Stapa, Talaibek Musaev, Natsue Hieda and Normalis Amzah

5. The in-depth interview as a research tool for investigating
   the online intercultural communication of Asian Internet users
   in relation to ethics in intercultural research   78
   Doris Fetscher

6. Are you an ELF? The relevance of ELF as an equitable social
   category in online intercultural communication   95
   Christopher Jenks

Index   109

Citation Information

The chapters in this book were originally published in *Language and Intercultural Communication*, volume 13, issue 1 (February 2013). When citing this material, please use the original page numbering for each article, as follows:

Introduction

Introduction: the discourse of ethics and equity
Shanta Nair-Venugopal
Language and Intercultural Communication, volume 13, issue 1 (February 2013)
pp. 1–9

Chapter 1

Intercultural ethics: questions of methods in language and intercultural communication
Alison Phipps
Language and Intercultural Communication, volume 13, issue 1 (February 2013)
pp. 10–26

Chapter 2

The uses of oral history in Cyprus: ethics, memory and identity
Holger Briel
Language and Intercultural Communication, volume 13, issue 1 (February 2013)
pp. 27–43

Chapter 3

Beyond the reach of ethics and equity? Depersonalisation and dehumanisation in foreign domestic helper narratives
Hans J. Ladegaard
Language and Intercultural Communication, volume 13, issue 1 (February 2013)
pp. 44–59

Chapter 4

Issues of language choice, ethics and equity: Japanese retirees living in Malaysia as their second home
Siti Hamin Stapa, Talaibek Musaev, Natsue Hieda and Normalis Amzah
Language and Intercultural Communication, volume 13, issue 1 (February 2013)
pp. 60–77

Chapter 5

The in-depth interview as a research tool for investigating the online intercultural communication of Asian Internet users in relation to ethics in intercultural research
Doris Fetscher
Language and Intercultural Communication, volume 13, issue 1 (February 2013)
pp. 78–94

Chapter 6

Are you an ELF? The relevance of ELF as an equitable social category in online intercultural communication
Christopher Jenks
Language and Intercultural Communication, volume 13, issue 1 (February 2013)
pp. 95–108

For any permission-related enquiries please visit:
http://www.tandfonline.com/page/help/permissions

Notes on Contributors

Normalis Amzah teaches Japanese language at the Foreign Languages and Translation Unit, National University of Malaysia, Bangi, Malaysia. She received her Bachelor of Business Administration from Nagoya University, Japan, and Master of Arts (Translation) from the University of Science Malaysia (USM).

Holger Briel is Director of the Media and Communication Programme at Xi'an Jiaotong Liverpool University, PRC. His most recent publication is *The Uses of Oral History: The Case of Cyprus* (2012), in which he explores the multifaceted usage of oral history in mapping contested communities. His research is focused on citizen media, intercultural phenomena, (Trans) Cultural Studies, Manga and Anime, broadcast media and changing visual regimes in the digital age, and the sociology of the digital world.

Doris Fetscher is Professor of Intercultural Training and Romance Cultures and Dean of the faculty of Applied Languages and Intercultural Communication at Zwickau's University of Applied Sciences, Germany. In 2000, she founded the Institute for Teacher Training and Intercultural Communication at the University of Augsburg, Germany, from which university she received her PhD in 2002. She has designed a master's degree program with a focus on intercultural project management in collaboration with universities in France and the Czech Republic. Her current research interests are in politeness and multilingualism.

Natsue Hieda is a Japanese language teacher at the Foreign Languages and Translation Unit, National University of Malaysia, Bangi, Malaysia. She received her Bachelor of Education degree from Toyama University, Japan, and her Master of Linguistics from the National University of Malaysia.

Christopher Jenks is an Assistant Professor of English at the University of South Dakota. His current research deals primarily with intercultural communication, world Englishes, English as a lingua franca, and discursive constructions of race. He is currently working on a book that examines race and ethnicity in the English language teaching profession in South Korea.

Hans J. Ladegaard is Professor and Head of the Department of English at the Hong Kong Polytechnic University. He studied at Odense University, Denmark and Cambridge University, UK, and taught at universities in Denmark and the UK before moving to Hong Kong in 2006. His research interests include intercultural/intergroup communication, language attitudes and stereotypes, language and gender, narratives of migration, and pragmatics and discourse analysis, and he has published widely on these issues in international journals and books. He is Co-Editor and Review Editor of *Pragmatics & Society* (John Benjamins).

Talaibek Musaev is a Senior Lecturer in the Faculty of Languages and Linguistics, University of Malaya, Kuala Lumpur, Malaysia. He received his PhD on International Communication from Nagoya University, Japan. His research interests are international communication, language discourse and applied linguistics. He currently teaches Japanese language, Japanese literature and discourse. He has published in the area of Japanese language education and teaching.

Shanta Nair-Venugopal is an Associate Fellow at the Institute of Malaysian and International Studies (IKMAS), National University of Malaysia/UKM where she was recently a guest scholar. She was previously Principal Fellow at the Institute of Occidental Studies, and prior to that Professor in the School of Language Studies and Linguistics, also at the National University of Malaysia/UKM. She has published internationally in the areas of language, discourse and intercultural communication in referred journals, books and other compilations. A more recent publication is *The Gaze of the West and Framings of the East* (Palgrave Macmillan, 2012).

Alison Phipps is Professor of Languages and Intercultural Studies at the University of Glasgow, UK, and co-Convener of the Glasgow Refugee, Asylum and Migration Network.

Siti Hamin Stapa is Professor in Applied Linguistics and Chair of the School of Language Studies and Linguistics, National University of Malaysia, Bangi, Malaysia. She received her PhD from Glasgow University, UK. Her research and teaching interests include written literacy and contrastive rhetoric. She has published in the area of applied linguistics.

INTRODUCTION

The discourse of ethics and equity

Shanta Nair-Venugopal

Institute of Occidental Studies, Universiti Kebangsaan Malaysia, Bangi, Malaysia

As the publication outcome of the International Association for Languages and Intercultural Communication (IALIC) symposium entitled 'The Discourse of Ethics and Equity in Language and Intercultural Communication', organized by the Institute of Occidental Studies, Universiti Kebangsaan Malaysia, from 9 to 10 December 2011 (for the first time outside Europe), this issue examines the notions of ethics and equity in relation to language, and intercultural communication and relations. Although predicated in the discourse of the field, these notions have not been addressed specifically either in a special issue of *LAIC* or an IALIC conference. This seems to be an omission given that much of the intercultural discourse and by extension the intercivilization dialogue of more recent times has been marked by reactions to Huntington's theses of a clash of civilizations (1993, 1996), and the almost prophetic bombings of 9/11, other subsequent 'terrorist' attacks and the indelible effects of these on equitable dealings between different peoples of the world, implicating tolerance, understanding, hospitality and safety.

In being used interchangeably with it, intercultural communication (ICC henceforth) appears to encompass the cross-cultural across borders. Yet bounded as it is by both natural and created borders and boundaries, the discourse also belongs to the minorities within (see Kramsch, 1998) – whether defined by the local, sub-fields or sub-cultures within the margins of territories, disciplines and communities. In a world of porous and dissolving borders and boundaries, of both state and non-state players, it is also the discourse of the glocal, the cosmopolitan and the a-cultural, and of universal rather than of distinctive or particular applicability. In embracing these dichotomies, the intercultural includes not only the space between cultures but also that occupied by similar groups (sub-cultures within a society). But none of these considerations free us from the responsibility of applying the restraints of ethics and equity, particularly in culturally dependent contexts and over what Ricouer refers to as 'historical time' (1985/88). It is to these restraints, which both constrain and empower ethics and equity, that this special issue is dedicated to.

In its early evolutionary days, the study of ICC as a type of communication, on both sides of the Atlantic, encompassed cross-cultural communication with a slavish preoccupation with difference. Given its long socio-history of intergroup relations fraught with difficulty, the US/American attempt to assimilate diverse groups of immigrants as citizens inevitably led to utilitarian or practical 'how to' studies, for instance, on how to accommodate, adjust or adapt as newcomers, rather than how to live socially integrated lives. As Park (1950, cited in Gudykunst, 1998, p. 77) notes ethnic diversity has traditionally been homogenised through a 'cycle of contact, competition, accommodation and eventual assimi-lation.' The cultures of similar groups were overgeneralized while differences between different groups were exaggerated. In such an approach, culture was conceived of as a problematic variable that interferes with the achievement of successful ICC. However, the preoccupation with difference also led fortuitously to the rehabilitation of the discourse of ICC (Gudykunst, 1998; Gudykunst & Kim, 1997; Hall, 1997; Wiseman, 1995) with deliberations on the notions of responsibility, ethics and equity as well (Casmir, 1997). Overlapping this rehabilitation were critiques of the predominant theoretical construct of culture as nation (see Ono, 2010), followed by work that argued for retheorizing culture as sites of struggle based on power relations and ideologies. These have given way to new and complex questions about culture and communication today.

In moving away from mainstream US/American functional approaches to ICC with the focus on interpersonal approaches that emphasized individual and group-centred attitudes and communication skills, Thomas Nakayama and Rona Halua-lani, in their impressive publication *The Handbook of Critical Intercultural Communication* (2010), offer a critical perspective of ICC. With reference to earlier work (Martin & Nakayama, 2000, cited in Nakayama & Halualani, 2010), it is defined as one that 'addresses issues of macro contexts (historical, social, and political levels), power, relevance, and the hidden and destabilizing aspects of culture' (p. 2) and which seeks to 'understand the role of power and contextual constraints on communication in order ultimately to achieve a more equitable society' (p. 8). They advocate that the full cycle of critical ICC moves as political projects from inquiry, to analysis, to reflection, to praxis and that ICC as a field goes 'beyond critique to sustained production of new knowledge on intercultural communication phenomena (and not just conceptualizations) based on a critical perspective' (Nakayama & Halualani, 2010, p. 11).

The British experience with ICC has emanated partly from being committed to finding an appropriate pedagogical response to the concern with culture in foreign language teaching too which had absorbed the Americans even more. In 1996, a group of scholars and practitioners (Mike Byram and associates) with an interest in the then fairly new concept of ICC gathered at Leeds Metropolitan University for the first in a series of conferences that resulted in the establishment of the International Association for Languages and Intercultural Communication (IALIC). This group included not only language teachers, but also scholars in management, anthropology, sociology, sociolinguistics and cultural studies, all of whom were keen to work in ICC. British scholars have since opened up the intercultural space by moving from (while maintaining) earlier initiatives in intercultural pedagogy to ideology (Holliday, 2010, 2011) to ethics (MacDonald & O'Regan, 2012) in critical engagement with the field. Indeed, in developing their own critical engagement of ethics in the field, through the work of Derrida and Levinas, MacDonald and O'Regan (2012) show, as Alison Phipps observes (this issue), 'how multiple selves, presences and others problematize transformational discourse and the assumption of difference as static or as overcome through intercultural work'. In asking to what extent a critical transformational discourse can refuse to engage in a transformational dialogue with these others, and (closely related to this) on what ethical grounds it might assert preference for its claims over the claims of these others, MacDonald and O'Regan (2012) propose a discourse ethics of responsibility that enables an intercultural praxis to engage critically and transformatively with regard to extreme cultural behaviour of the other.

The European experience in ICC has been galvanized with the formation of the EU and has assumed importance in educational and professional domains particularly those of business and management with the impact of globalization and transnational movements of various kinds. The integration of Europe as a mixed polity marked by different degrees of human mobility, the cultural interpenetration of its different societies and the geopolitics of its changing relations of centres to peripheries (see Beck & Delanty, 2006) have augmented that experience. The European intercultural space has been widened considerably now with the emerging discourse of cosmopolitanism as new thinking that shadows interculturalism in the intercultural praxis of citizenship in the 'integrated Europe' of a supra-national EU. Similarly, the global experience has been to confront the onslaught of notions of monolithic 'national cultures' (Hofstede, 1984/2001, 1991/2005), especially the essentialism of individualism and collectivism (McSweeney, 2002; see also Para-masivam & Nair-Venugopal, 2012), and the parochialism of cultural relativism, including fledging attempts at extending a framework of ICC (see Nair-Venugopal, 2003). The irony is not lost on many at a time of post-Western European cosmopolitanism that the reified labels of individualism and collectivism come from the West. A 'geography of thought' (Nisbett, 2003) has even described different ways of thinking between so-called Westerners and Asians as a clash of mentalities, close on the heels of Huntington's clash of civilizations theses.

In many ways, it is the anthropologist Michael Lambek who sets the tone for this issue with the affirmation in his 2010 volume *Ordinary Ethics*, that human beings as a species are fundamentally ethical, 'given our consciousness, our socialization and sociality, and our use of language' and argues that the forces that shape human action start with ethics; 'that ethics is intrinsic to speech and action'. The call for 'ordinary ethics' he submits echoes the arguments of Wittgenstein and Austin with respect to 'ordinary language' where

> we may find the wellsprings of ethical insight deeply embedded in the categories and functions of languages and ways of speaking, in the common sense ways we distinguish among various kinds of actors or characters, kinds of acts and manners of acting; in specific nouns and adjectives, verbs and adverbs, or adverbial phrases respectively; thus, in the shared criteria we use to make ourselves intelligible to one another, in 'what we say when'. (p. 2)

That seemed an endorsement of part of what we sought to address as ethics in the discourse of language and ICC in the Malaysian symposium. As a modality of social action, ethics is universal, yet particularistic as a property, dimension and function of the intention to act. The importance and place of ethics in ICC appears to be most significant at the juncture where individuals as social actors, either as the 'stranger' (Harman, 1988; Simmel, 1971) or as the 'cultural other', 'interact'. We are reminded that 'cosmopolitanism' is ethics in a world of strangers (Appiah, 2006). Mindful of what we say and when we say what we say also evokes for many who work in, and with, the English language, for instance, the linguistic ethics of Austin, Searle and Grice, and the cultural ethics of Malinowski, Hymes and Hall, notwithstanding recent critiques. More recent work in intercultural ethics (Evanoff, 2004, 2006) has looked at universalist, relativist and constructivist approaches, and integration, respectively.

Neither Eastern nor Western in its universality, yet both Eastern and Western in its particularity, ethics evokes both a foundational and implicit appeal to transcendental morality or theism. Indigenous religions have provided the bases of ontological morality. We are reminded, for instance, of the five Buddhist principles of peaceful coexistence, *Pancasila*, and the Middle Way; the Hindu discipline of action, *Karma Yoga*, and of non-violence, *Ahimsa*; Christian charity and unconditional love of neighbour, and moral responsibility in Islam, *akhlaq*, which embraces a vocabulary of ethics. Human society as a whole also values keeping one's word as indicative of one's honour, which leads to respect and the enactment of human dignity. It is in its susceptibility to the vagaries of the treatment of people irrespective of social or cultural differences, that ethics is either equitable or not as Hans Ladegaard argues in this issue.

With regard to equity (as social justice), Charles Taylor (1994) notes in his seminal essay on the politics of multiculturalism, that equality with regard to the notion of recognition was an important trajectory historically in the movement from the ideal of honour to that of dignity, which came about with the decline of hierarchical societies. Taylor observes that democracy, which has taken various forms over the years (such as the more recent developments of the Arab Spring) in ushering in a politics of equal recognition, has 'now returned in the form of demands for the equal status of cultures and genders' (1994, p. 27). And in order to understand the close link between identity and recognition, he argues that one has to understand that 'the crucial feature of human life is its fundamental dialogical character'; that people do not acquire the languages needed for self-definition on their own but are introduced to them through interaction with others who matter; the 'significant others' of George Herbert Mead (1935, cited in Taylor, 1994, p. 32). Within the presumed homogeneity of the intracultural space occupied by similar groups, the 'significant other' is an important dialogical influence in the process of enculturation. However, in the intercultural space of contestations occupied by different groups, the dialogue is frequently one between minorities and the majority, as Holger Briel, Hans Ladegaard and Siti Hamin Stapa et al. demonstrate in this issue. And while 'meaning may be generated in intercultural encounters just as easily as in intracultural encounters...the amount of shared meaning may vary dramatically' (Hall, 1997, p. 31) giving rise to inequitable and 'missed' communication.

Inequitable attitudes to language and communication have been observed with regard to language choice and use in the workplace as a natural site of ICC, given its social borders; how the emphasis on a type of linguistic normativity disadvantages many; how establishment views and corporate talk and institutional directives as business discourse create an aura of dependency in the ideology of an idealized, abstract linguistic norm that is unattainable to many in the local workplace and even more increasingly, non-essential (Nair-Venugopal, 2009). Furthermore, in valorizing the value-addedness of standardized language competence as one of the golden keys to global economic competitiveness, the employment chances of legions of potential recruits from diverse linguistic backgrounds are also stymied. Treating language as a commodity, rather than as a resource, virtually shuts out those for whom language is an innate authentic talent, that is, variable, situated and contextualized as Monica Heller argues (2003, 2010). In such scenarios, the discourse of interculturality is that of authenticity versus the commodification of standardized language use. Ethics and equity are clearly implicated if faith in the potential productive capacity of the linguistic and cultural diversity of the workforce of a society is not restored because the language of work should work for everyone by freeing the linguistically oppressed from the imposition of normativity, as Paulo Freire (1970) might argue.

Participants to the symposium were invited to elaborate on similar and other scenarios and triggered to respond to why some groups of individuals, like fund managers, celebrities and well-heeled tourists (no matter what language they speak), are inevitably better 'understood' than others like refugees, trafficked persons, and marginalized communities and individuals? We raised the philosophical question of whether the intention to understand and 'tolerate' is as important as the intention to 'accept' and understand? The six contributors to this issue responded with a range of papers that explore and address these and attendant questions.

Firstly, Alison Phipps traces the development of methodology in language and ICC in an impressive sweep of the literature to reveal a problematic basis with its ethical considerations. She argues that although the focus on difference and solution orientations to intercultural conflict has been a fundamental driver for theory, data collection and methods in the field, and has created a considerable consciousness raising industry, with methods, trainings and 'critical incidents', these ultimately focus intellectual energy in areas which, while they may be productive in terms of courses and publications, implicate questions of ethics. Drawing on the dual aporias identified by MacDonald and O'Regan (2012), Holliday's 'spaces' for the visibility of margins and 'decentred' research (2009), Woitsch's 'intercultural walks' (2011) and especially Tuhiwai Smith's decolonized research methodologies (2010), Phipps decries methodology in the field with an impassioned plea for decolonized, decentred, restorative, collaborative, participatory, sensory, even healing methodologies of creativity and artistry as intercultural poetics.

In the next paper, Holger Briel considers the problem of ethics in the telling of stories in an Oral History (OH) or 'living memory' project undertaken from 2009 to 2012 in Cyprus by enabling voices that may be ignored in the dominant political discourse to be heard. Briel sees the role of ethics as a very important area of inquiry in OH. It extends for him beyond interviewer and interviewee relationships to interview set ups, interviewer and interviewee selections, questionnaire/interview design and post-interviews, analysis and the dissemination of information to one of the main dilemmas of OH research – questions of truth versus securing 'a good' interview. He identifies ethics, visuality, identity and memory as the backbone of OH. Given the political volatility of a Turkish-Cypriot north and a Greek-Cypriot-dominated south, the project's hope was to empower the respondents and enhance their understanding of the historic processes that have shaped and continue to shape their lives and the ethics of living on a divided island. It attempted firstly to find ways in which both sides of the divide might be able to re-approach each other by claiming a common past. Secondly, it attempted to find common intercultural and ethical language that individuals could use to talk about their past, especially the good times of shared daily lives and how these memories could be used to build a common future to overcome intercultural misunderstandings and conflicts which is a province of ethics.

In the third paper, Hans Ladegaard appeals for research commitment and social commitment to be upheld in projects that involve marginalized and underprivileged groups (citing Solis, 2004 and Shuman, 2005) by advocating that research on domestic helper narratives should not just be *on* foreign domestic helpers (FDHs), but also *for* and *with* them (after Cameron et al., 1992). In attempting to represent intercultural discourses that seem to move beyond the reach of ethics and equity, Ladegaard makes a compelling case as the socially committed researcher for the silenced voice of the abused FDH; that it is beyond the pale of ethics and equity and evacuates both notions from the discursive space. He employs the social constructionist framework in which the researcher as the social activist situates and coconstructs the interaction with the participant. Although we are mindful of the arguments in social science research against insider subjectivity, Ladegaard argues that a critical intercultural scholar is inherently political, seeing himself as a social activist; that the two roles may be complimentary rather than contradictory. The concept of ontologization (after Tileaga, 2007) is employed to help explain and understand how certain groups become conceptualized as legitimate outcasts.

Siti Hamin Stapa et al. discuss foreign minorities too in the fourth paper, but as a privileged group of fairly well-heeled retirees from Japan living 'the good life' in Malaysia as a second home under a government initiative called the MM2H programme. Two issues are investigated in relation to this group. The first is that of the preferred language choice of the retirees. The findings from a survey suggest that English was the majority choice for both informal and formal interactions. It is inferred that they are not motivated to learn local languages although quite clearly that would facilitate deeper contacts with the locals enhancing intercultural understanding. Based on the findings, considerations of ethics and equity underlying the language preferences were examined as the retirees clearly positioned themselves as sojourners residing in Malaysia principally to enjoy the economic benefits of retirement rather than as permanent residents. Siti Hamin Stapa et al. label this unique situation as *contemplation*, based on observation of the emotional adaptation of the retirees to the new environment. Their personal needs are taken care of either by Japanese agents or in locating a 'little Japan' in Malaysia for themselves. Because it focuses on the economic aspects of the partnership, the programme does not seek to provide intercultural opportunities or benefits and allows instead for the retirees to live comfortably but in social isolation from the wider Malaysian society. With limited language ability in both English and local languages, they fail to create social networks with the locals. This impinges on the ethics and equity of their interactions with locals and their social exclusion.

The last two papers deal with computer-mediated communication (CMC). Doris Fetscher looks at messages posted on the Internet and Christopher Jenks at interactions in chat rooms. Both are concerned with categories relevant to research; Fetscher with intercultural problems and cultural differences, and Jenks with the social category of English as lingua franca (ELF).

Doris Fetscher argues, in the penultimate paper of this issue, that since virtual ICC is of great interest in intercultural research, it is moot to find out how a researcher can gain access to this field of investigation if s/he does not or only partially speaks the languages of the subjects. Following Cheong, Martin, and Macfadyen's aspiration in *New Media and Intercultural Communication* (2012), to foreground 'primary *ethical* impulses . . . in both the potentially salutary as well as the potentially destructive impacts of CMC; namely, a foundational sense of responsibility for "the Other"' (p. xvii), Fetscher asks two hierarchically related research questions based on the argument that to disregard the users' cultural background, that is, multiple, complex and culturally variable beliefs, practices, norms and sense of identity, is a 'form of violence against the Other' (p. xvii). The questions are whether the in-depth interview is a suitable tool for gaining insights into the virtual multilingual environments and communicative practices of German-speaking colleagues of Asian descent and which intercultural problems and cultural differences are relevant to the interview partners, and how they make them relevant. The study demonstrates through postings by German and German-speaking Filipina, Taiwanese and Korean users of the Internet that categories relevant to research can be accessed through in-depth interviews to generate an interactive awareness process that both partners contribute to equally and which comply with the requirements of intercultural research ethics in CMC research.

In the last paper in this issue, Christopher Jenks reviews different social categories that are made relevant when geographically dispersed speakers of English as an additional language communicate in the global context and virtual space of chat rooms. He examines the extent to which interactants see themselves as lingua franca speakers on the basis of a claim that the literature characterizes them as such, which implicates issues of linguistic hegemony and unequal power relations. Membership categorization analysis is used to investigate how social categories related to English are enacted in, and through, talk and interaction in language proficiency compliments, language proficiency talk, and getting acquainted sequences. The findings reveal that English as a lingua franca is not a social category that is made relevant at all during the chats. Those that are made relevant are 'foreigner', 'language learner' and 'non-native' as identity constructions in relation to speaking English. On the basis of these observations, Jenks argues for an equitable, impartial and context-sensitive approach to examining identities in ICC that proscribes social categories a priori, and explores the validity of using the term English as a lingua franca (ELF) as interactants demonstrate that they possess, and make relevant, a number of different social categories in speaking English.

All the contributors to this issue have been in tune with the tone and narrative of the theme of the symposium in exploring and excavating for discussion related issues of either ethics or equity, or both, in a spread of six papers that have looked at marginalized and privileged minorities, victims of abuse and of conflict, researchers and practitioners, language learners and speaker/users as the subjects of the discourse. The hope is that some of the spaces in the discourse on ethics and equity in language and ICC have now been opened up for readers of *LAIC* to incite them into action in the production of 'new knowledge' in language and ICC.

Acknowledgements

I wish to thank each and every one of the reviewers for so generously finding the time to review the papers they accepted.

References

Appiah, A. (2006). *Cosmopolitanism: Ethics in a world of strangers.* New York: Norton.

Beck, U., & Delanty, G. (2006). Europe from a cosmopolitan perspective. In G. Delanty (Ed.), *Europe and Asia beyond East and West* (pp. 11–23). New York: Routledge.

Casmir, F.L. (1997). *Ethics in intercultural and international communication.* Mahwah, NJ: Lawrence Erlbaum.

Evanoff, R. (2004). Universalist, relativist, and constructivist approaches to intercultural ethics. *International Journal of Intercultural Relations, 28,* 439–458.

Evanoff, R. (2006). Integration in intercultural ethics. *International Journal of Intercultural Relations, 30,* 421–437.

Freire, P. (1970). *Pedagogy of the oppressed.* New York: Continuum Press.

Gudykunst, W.B. (1998). *Bridging differences: Effective intergroup communication.* Thousand Oaks, CA: Sage.

Gudykunst, W.B., & Kim, Y.Y. (1997). *Communicating with strangers: An approach to intercultural communication.* Boston: McGraw-Hill.

Hall, B.J. (1997). Culture, ethics and communication. In F.L. Casmir (Ed.), *Ethics in intercultural and international communication.* Mahwah, NJ: Lawrence Erlbaum.

Harman, L. (1988). *The modern stranger: On language and membership.* Berlin: Mouton de Gruyter.

Heller, M. (2003). Globalization, the new economy and the commodification of language and identity. *Journal of Sociolinguistics, 7*(4), 473–492.

Heller, M. (2010). Language as resource in the globalized new economy. In N. Coupland (Ed.), *Handbook of language and globalisation* (pp. 349–365). Oxford: Wiley-Blackwell.

Hofstede, G. (1984/2001). *Culture's consequences: International differences in work related values/Comparing values, behaviours, institutions, and organisations across nations.* Beverly Hills, CA: Sage.

Hofstede, G. (1991/2005). *Cultures and organizations: Software of the mind/Intercultural cooperation and its importance for survival.* London: McGraw-Hill.

Holliday, A. (2010). Cultural descriptions as political acts: An exploration. *Language and Intercultural Communication, 10*(3), 259–272.

Holliday, A. (2011). *Intercultural communication and ideology.* London: Sage.

Huntington, S. (1993). The clash of civilizations? *Foreign Affairs, 72*(3), 22–49.

Huntington, S. (1996). *The clash of civilizations and the remaking of world order.* New York: Simon and Schuster.

Kramsch, C. (1998). *Language and culture.* Oxford: Oxford University Press.

Lambek, M. (Ed.). (2010). *Ordinary ethics: Anthropology, language, and action.* New York: Fordham University Press.

MacDonald, M., & O'Regan, J.P. (2012). The ethics of intercultural communication. *Educational Philosophy & Theory.* Advance online publication. doi: 10.1111/j.1469-5812. 2011.00833.x

McSweeney, B. (2002). Hofstede's model of national cultural differences and their consequences: A triumph of faith – A failure of analysis. *Human Relations, 55*(1), 89–118.

Nair-Venugopal, S. (2003). Approximations of social reality as interpretations of culture: Extending a framework of analysis in intercultural communication. *Journal of International Communication, 9*(2), 13–28.

Nair-Venugopal, S. (2009). Localised perspectives: Malaysia. In F. Bargiela-Chiappini (Ed.), *Handbook of business discourse* (pp. 387–399). Edinburgh: Edinburgh University Press.

Nakayama, T., & Halualani, R. (Eds.). (2010). *The handbook of critical intercultural communication.* Oxford: Wiley-Blackwell.

Nisbett, R. (2003). *The geography of thought.* New York: Free Press.

Ono, K. (2010). Reflections on 'Problematizing "nation" in intercultural communication research'. In T.K. Nakayama & R.T. Halualani (Eds.), *The handbook of critical intercultural communication* (pp. 84–97). Oxford: Wiley-Blackwell.

Paramasivam, S., & Nair-Venugopal, S. (2012). Indian collectivism revisited: Unpacking the Western gaze. In S. Nair-Venugopal (Ed.), *The gaze of the West and framings of the East.* Basingstoke: Palgrave Macmillan.

Ricouer, P. (1985/88). *Time and narrative* [Temps et Récit] (K. McLaughlin & D. Pellauer, Trans.). 3 vols. Chicago: University of Chicago Press.

Simmel, G. (1971). The stranger. In D. Levine (Ed.), *Individuality and forms* (pp. 43–149). Chicago: University of Chicago Press.

Taylor, C. (1994). The politics of recognition. In A. Gutmann (Ed.), *Multiculturalism: Examining the politics of recognition*. Princeton, NJ: Princeton University Press.

Wiseman, R.L. (1995). *Intercultural communication theory*. Thousands Oaks, CA: Sage.

Intercultural ethics: questions of methods in language and intercultural communication

Alison Phipps

School of Education, University of Glasgow, Glasgow, UK

This paper explores how questions of ethics and questions of method are intertwined and unavoidable in any serious study of language and intercultural communication. It argues that the focus on difference and solution orientations to intercultural conflict has been a fundamental driver for theory, data collection and methods in the field. These approaches, the paper argues, have created a considerable consciousness raising industry, with methods, trainings and 'critical incidents', which ultimately focus intellectual energy in areas which may be productive in terms of courses and publications but which have a problematic basis in their ethical terrain.

Dieser Artikel untersucht wie ethische und methodische Fragen nicht nur ineinander greifen, sondern in keiner ernstzunehmenden Studie ueber Sprache und interkulturelle Kommunikation ausgelassen werden duerfen. Es wird hier argumentiert, dass der Schwerpunkt auf Verschiedenheit und Problemorientierung im interkulturellen Konflikt einen wesentlichen Einfluss auf theoretische Entwicklungen, Datenerhebung und Methoden in diesem Bereich hatte. Dieser Artikel legt auch dar, wie diese Ansaetze eine betraechtliche 'Bewusstseinsbildungs – Branche' erzeugt haben, mit Methoden, Trainings, und 'kritischen Interaktionssituationen', welche letztendlich allen intellektuellen Arbeitseifer auf Bereiche konzentriert hat, die zwar ertragreich sind in Bezug auf Kurse und Publikationen, jedoch eine problematische Grundlage im ethischen Bereich aufweisen.

Introducing intercultural ethics

From the vantage point of the colonized, a position from which I write and choose to privilege, the term 'research' is inextricably linked to European imperialism and colonialism. The word itself, 'research' is probably one of the dirtiest words in the indigenous world's vocabulary. When mentioned in many indigenous contexts, it stirs up silence, it conjures up bad memories, it raises a smile that is knowing and distrustful. It is so powerful that indigenous people even write poetry about research. (Tuhiwai Smith, 2012, p. 1)

How might good intercultural relationships be developed which do not provoke or perpetuate such statements about research? How can good intercultural language teaching and learning be fostered and how might good intercultural research take place? Who judges how good this is and against which criteria? On first reading, these questions may appear to be concerned with the functional issue of quality assurance in intercultural language education – how it is that the profession of intercultural language educators ensures that standards are in place and benchmarks are attained, that the research undertaken is done in a satisfactory manner. Much energy has been spent in recent years on such questions of quality and the development of frameworks for intercultural language education. In Europe, the Common European Framework of Reference has given rise to a set of standards and approaches to intercultural language pedagogy which have found resonance world-wide (Byram & Parmenter, 2012). Similarly, in a variety of national and international research contexts, sets of standards have been elaborated with regard to the good conduct of empirical research with human subjects. This work has unfolded in national settings and in accordance with national laws and policies regarding the nature of research and education. The questions of good intercultural relationships, language pedagogy and good intercultural research are also questions of ethics, pertaining to what constitutes just relationships, what might be virtues in the conduct of intercultural research, how teaching might be done in such a way as to enable human flourishing, restorative research relationships and where research is not one of the 'dirtiest of words' and the experience lends itself to a different kind of poetics altogether.

Classical literature provides an initial starting point for their discussion, most notably Aristotle's *Nicomachean Ethics*. It is in this classical, even founding text, of philosophical ethics that we find interconnections between aesthetics and ethics. Aristotle points out that the things 'that are beautiful and just, about which politics investigates, involve great disagreement and inconsistency, so that they are thought to belong only to convention and not to nature' (2002, p. 2). 'Things that are beautiful and just' are grouped together here creating an implicit relationship between what is deemed to be aesthetically pleasing and what is understood as ethical. The question of ethics cannot be uncoupled from the aesthetics and symbols of the actions in question. For Aristotle this relationship is not described as one between two discrete abstracts but rather as a method, 'all making, investigating (every methodos, like the Ethics itself), all deliberate actions and choice, all aim at some good. [...] there is one highest aim, happiness.' Ethics, here, are deliberate actions, makings, methods. It is not so much a state or imposition as a common process of becoming and creating.

In this paper, I wish to explore the relationship between ethics and aesthetics as it has developed in language and intercultural communication and to consider what bearing this relationship has for decolonizing research methods in the field. In an important article in this journal in 2009, Holliday discusses the 'connection between Centre dominance and the need for professionals and academics to assert their status through the defining of speakerhood, culture and language within purportedly neutral technical or scientific categories'. Holliday argues that:

> This is not an evil plot to dominate the world – just a modernist attempt to rationalise and make things work. However, even within the cosmopolitanism of new thinking it is hard to move on from these powerful devices for advancing practice and knowledge. The solution seems not to lie within the sensitising and liberalising of Centre thinking, but with a cessation of the zealous defining and fixing of others in order to allow spaces for the margins to become visible. (2009, p. 153)

Following on from Holliday's conclusions, this paper is concerned with the question of how it is that research methods in language and intercultural communication can rise to the considerable challenge of 'ceasing their zealous defining and fixing of others in order to allow spaces for the margins to become visible'. For me, this is centrally a question of intercultural ethics and aesthetics in the practice of research. In order to address this aspect of research in language and intercultural communication I first trace ethical concerns in the field. I then examine deconstructivist critiques of the field and of the assumed ethical positions moving to consider the possibility of intercultural ethics in research methods which allow spaces for the margins to become visible in ways which trace Aristotle's view of ethics as inherently linked to aesthetics.

Tracing an ethics of awareness in language and intercultural communication

The field of language and intercultural communication as a critical endeavour developed, in part, out of the cross-cultural capability conferences held in Leeds in the mid- to late 1990s. It offered a theoretical and conceptual space for the development of critical, postcolonial approaches to questions of language and intercultural communication. The concept of 'capability' grew out of Sen and Nussbaum's work on human development (Nussbaum & Sen, 1993) and was seen to offer a broader development than competency-based models, then in the ascendency. In the early conferences of the International Association of Languages and Intercultural Communication a critical strand of work relating to ethics was discernible in both theoretical debates and with respect to methods of language pedagogy (Killick, Parry, & Phipps, 2001a, 2001b; Thurlow, 2002).

Some of this work built on paradigms of critical pedagogy, notably those of Paulo Freire (1970) and Henry Giroux (1988, 1992), to develop a conceptual ethics for intercultural education, which could trace roots back to the liberatory movements of the 1960s and 1970s and which was influenced by struggles against apartheid in South Africa and US Civil Rights movements. The intercultural ethics in play concerned activism in the face of injustice and prejudice, incorporation of postcolonial critiques, and teaching and learning intercultural communication and intercultural communicative competence in such a way as to engender considered action and engagement in specific issues of human development. Focus was on theory, largely from poststructuralist and critical humanist paradigms, and on methods for language teaching, in particular, communicative methods and critiques therefore (for a full review, see Kumaravadivelu, 2006). What was deemed to be 'good' was what was liberatory, in a democratic and political sense, and what worked to foster awareness in the increasingly intercultural language classrooms of Europe. This work took intercultural language education beyond communicative methods, critical incidents and tolerance or awareness, or even empathy, to an engaged pedagogy of intercultural action in ethical and political matters. In this, intercultural language research shared common cause with postcolonial studies and other critical movements in the humanities and social scientific research.

Of significance in this critical strand of work is the work of Gavin Jack (Jack, 2009; Jack & Lorbiecki, 2003). Jack proposed a Foucaultian discursive approach from a position of critique of management ethics of profitability. Through analyses of labour markets and globalization, Jack demonstrates the extent of the ethical divides between intercultural managers and intercultural labourers in a variety of contexts. The ethical assumption in the work of many of these scholars was that intercultural communication and work towards its realization should proceed along lines of democracy and equality and that these were often incompatible with dominant economic rationale or systems of global corporate governance. Others also laid foundations for an intercultural identity ethic at this time, notably Crawshaw (Crawshaw, Callen, & Tusting, 2001) through his work on identity, 'ipseité' and Ricoeur, and Parry (Parry 2003) and her Bergsonian humanist stance which considered the place of the arts and creativity in the work of intercultural language education and identity formation. In more recent years, these critical and engaged perspectives have been enhanced by postcolonial and occidental studies, notably in the work of Nair-Venugopal (2009, 2012) and Adejunmobi (2004).

Creativity and poetics as aesthetic concerns were brought into dialogue with social scientific data on intercultural language education and a plurality of methodological experimentation in language and intercultural research is represented in the proceedings of the early conferences, which provided the foundation for this journal (Byram, Nichols, & Stevens, 2001; Cronin, 2002; Killick et al., 2001a, 2001b; Parry, 2003). The work of literary authors from postcolonial contexts was a feature of the attempts, unsystematic and experimental as they were in the early conferences, to open a space for narrative and for data to speak from beyond the confines of the forms defined by the research interview and the notion of the 'informant', the tape recorder or the codifications in NVivo or SPS. Poetry, drama, visual media, and biography and autobiography were found in the conference proceedings in a moment of critical possibility and openness, facilitated by the conference chairs, Margaret Parry and David Killick, which fostered such exploration (Cormeraie, Parry, & Killick, 2000). This work stood as its own poetic redress to the dominant social scientific methods at work in the various subfields of language and intercultural research. It did not claim to advance its own methodologies for research but rather to act as a site for research in and of itself. From this work came studies of the intercultural narrative and of literary translation as a locus for the analysis of the intercultural imagination (Crawshaw et al., 2001; Cronin, 2000).

At the same time as these theoretical and ethical concerns were emerging in the field, a large body of work on practical instances of classroom solutions to awareness raising was being developed, where awareness acted as an ethical imperative. Through all of this work is the assumption that intercultural encounter brings possibilities but also creates problems and conflict and that awareness raising is the key to conflict prevention, with some of this material aiming at engaging controversial issues or aspects of social life. In the UK, increasingly language classroom practice was being shaped through ethnographic and experiential critical models of learning and students' work was brought to the fore in papers which suggested the cycles of experience and reflection were successful in raising awareness of intercultural matters (Corbett, 2003, 2010; Roberts, Byram, Barro, Jordan, & Street, 2001). There was a rich description in the work of this time of classrooms alight with awareness and exploration of intercultural issues and their place in language pedagogy. Early work in the series Languages for Intercultural Communication and Education, published by Multilingual Matters, showcased examples of this work, notably in *Developing Intercultural Communication in Practice* (Byram et al., 2001), which have now become mainstream in the teaching of intercultural language pedagogy in the UK and beyond. These offer instances of the kinds of 'postmethod pedagogy' discussed at length by Kumaravadivelu (2001, 2012a, 2012b) though the dominance of communicative models of language pedagogy has yet to be challenged or to be seen as practical in contexts of the global south outwith the central concerns of liberal democratic models of critical pedagogy (Akbari, 2008).

In more recent years, work on ethics has come in the form of concepts of 'intercultural responsibility' and through Guilherme's leadership of the ICOPROMO and INTERACT projects (Guilherme, Glaser, & Mendez-Garcia, 2010). Both these projects afforded the opportunity to gather empirical data which would enable training and interaction in intercultural responsibility as one strand of the research projects. Intercultural responsibility is an important development as it offers a framework of voice, global ethics and solidarity which work within conceptualization and critiques of globalization, democracy and human rights. This work is influenced by Ting Toomey's interpersonal and individualized models of intercultural commu- nication which propose mindfulness and consciousness levels as the ground upon which attitudes may be changed and responsibility assumed (1999). To this we might add the work of Holmes (2011) on dialogical ethics and interfaith discourse and Byram (2008b), also Starkey's later work on citizenship and human rights which also works with notions of intercultural citizenship, cosmopolitanism and tolerance (2007). In this work we see scholars based in Europe and North America grappling with the critiques and limits of modernist Human Rights discourse and of the challenges brought by the dominant political concerns with security in the wake of the terrorist attacks of September 11, 2001. To this we might add the work of Dervin (2012) and his discussion of the need for interculturally competent researchers who seriously research with rather than on their subjects. Together with many other contributions too numerous to list here, we see the emergence of a critical discourse which has emerged during this period to challenge the dominant hegemony of English language scholarship and English language conceptual dominance – though not quite taking the path of Ngugi wa Thiong'o (1986), especially in his Kikuyu writings, or Maírín nic Eoinn's *Trén bhFearann Breac* (2005) in her commitment to Irish scholarship in Irish, both examples of scholars exploring the research life of their mother tongues.

Two aporias: debating the theoretical basis for ethics in language and intercultural communication

At work in much of the development of intercultural language research has been what MacDonald and O'Regan (2012) carefully excavate and identify as two aporias. Firstly, they identify 'an unstated impetus towards a universal consciousness;- assumed as universally given'. As such the work of the late 1990s reflected the possibilities of largely North American, Australasian and European scholars, engaging in this strand of work at the time, to enjoy degrees of freedom of expression and intercultural engagement not shared universally worldwide, yet aspired to from within liberal, democratic societies and promoted by the methods of teaching and of research available to such scholars. It is true that such labour, in terms of teaching and research, is something of a luxury and requires certain conditions of security and material possibility to be formulated (Bourdieu, 2000). Critics go as far as seeing such thinking as potentially imperial, exclusive and unethical in their then lack of incorporation of perspectives from the global south in particular, and in languages outwith the European Centre of French, German and English. The verdict: could do better; try harder; learn more languages; listen; do intercultural research according to the values and 'competences' of intercultural education (Dervin, 2012).

Secondly, their argument demonstrates how the truth claims of much of intercultural communication discourse are grounded in an 'implicit appeal to a transcendental moral signified'. In short, what MacDonald and O'Regan demonstrate in their important article is the way the aims and objectives of intercultural curricular and materials aim at presuming an implicit ethic of awareness as universally held and tending towards universalizing solutions in either critical transformation or pragmatic solution, through its 'metaphysics of presence'. They also show the extent to which this consciousness is a presumed ethic of intercultural awareness, moving towards notions of harmony, tolerance, citizenship and democracy, which are assumed universals of human rights, and presented as unproblematically given and shared. In short they characterize a situation ripe for renewed critical engagement.

Developing their own ethical engagement through the work of Derrida and Levinas (op. cit.), MacDonald and O'Regan (2012) show how multiple selves, presences and others problematize transformational discourse and the assumption of difference as static or as overcome through intercultural work. They ask: 'To what extent can a critical transformational discourse refuse to engage in a transformational dialogue with these others; and closely related to this, on what ethical grounds might it assert preference for its claims over the claims of these others?' (p. 5).

MacDonald and O'Regan's work echoes an early contribution to the field by Peter Cryle (2002). In this piece, 'Should We Stop Worrying about Cultural Awareness?', Cryle identifies a 'prestige of theories of consciousness' in which he sees a danger that scholars in the field of intercultural studies 'will be caught up indefinitely with intriguing, yet unproductive questions' and asks 'whether the notional of cultural awareness deserves our full attention, and our enduring professional commitment?' (p. 24).

An example of precisely this colonizing prestige of consciousness in action, from the field of anthropology, is exemplified by the work of Lila Abu-Lughod (2002) in her article 'Do Muslim Women Really Need Saving? Anthropological Reflections on Cultural Relativism and its Others'. This article enacts precisely the same concerns regarding the prestige of consciousness and of the dual aporias identified by MacDonald and O'Regan. Abu-Lughod complains of the way Western feminism tends to construct veiling as a problematic practice of difference which should not be accepted but overcome, and from which Muslim women need 'saving'. Her conclusions regarding veiling are similar to those of MacDonald and O'Regan and enact a structure of respect which allows for different even incompatible understandings of identity, difference and practice of faith to coexist.

What I am advocating is the hard work involved in recognizing and respecting differences – precisely as products of different histories, as expressions of different circumstances, and as manifestations of differently structured desires. We may want justice for women, but can we accept that there might be different ideas about justice and that different women might want, or choose, different futures from what we envision as best (see Ong 1988)? We must consider that they might be called to personhood, so to speak, in a different language.

Could we not leave veils and vocations of saving others behind and instead train our sights on ways to make the world a more just place? (Abu-Lughod, 2002, p. 789)

Cryle and Abu-Lughod are both concerned with the way intercultural and critical studies appear to have a knack of creating unproductive questions and sidestepping questions of engagement and justice. A 'good' life, in Aristotle's aesthetic and ethical terms, may be a life as a Muslim woman as one of a variety of identities. Visible, aural, tangible differences jolt the senses but this jolting does not require an education programme in awareness or a critical campaign to transform. However complex these discussions are and however many views it is clear that traditional prestige assumptions or methods of eliciting opinions are woefully inadequate when judged ethically. Instead, there is a different, ethical–political task which emerges, which is far more consonant with the methods which indigenous and critical intercultural researchers have adopted in recent years: the practice of listening, naming, reclaiming, co-creating, participating, sharing. Such practices are carefully rooted in relationships and forms of relating which require receiving the other in their personhood and with their habitation practices as they are.

It is therefore to a theory of methods that I wish to turn in order to suggest a way out of the dual theoretical aporias identified cogently by MacDonald and O'Regan.

Questions of research methods

The work reviewed above advances the early ethical propositions in the field and charts their development from the Marxist and modernist frameworks of the early 1990s into a poststructuralist and globalized conceptualization. That said, there is an assumption in this work that ethical intercultural relationships occur at the level of consciousness, awareness raising and of concepts such as democracy and tolerance and citizenship. The classroom approaches emerging under these framings of ethics in intercultural language pedagogy involve expanded teaching and training modules, action at the level of each individual learner through the development of portfolios of evidence of changed and transformed attitudes and through the move to create a range of standards for intercultural competence, which included the work on the UK National Occupation Standards in Intercultural Working (Lund & O'Regan, 2010; MacDonald, O'Regan, & Witana, 2009). They represent, what Kumaravadivelu (2001) terms 'postmethod pedagogy' – a pedagogy focusing not so much on a universal method of communicative language teaching, but one which has seen:

> [an] overarching transition in terms of three principal and perceptible shifts: (a) from communicative language teaching to taskbased language teaching, (b) from method-based pedagogy to postmethod pedagogy, and (c) from systemic discovery to critical discourse. (Kumaravadivelu, 2006, p. 60)

These aspects of postmethod pedagogy present themselves as curricular facets of globalization and internationalization, preparing teachers and students to engage in a co-constructive, decentring and critical way with people who are not the same in terms of class or ethnicity or linguistic background or nationally as a result of the transnational movement of labour, people and capital that have come with what Bauman (2000) terms 'liquid modernity' and Pennycook (2007), following Appadurai (1996), refers to as 'global flows'. In order to engage with liquid modernity, certain ethical and political theoretical and pedagogic approaches are clearly required, which will enable negotiation of contradictory elements.

Whilst considerable advances have been made towards the development of co-productive, exploratory, postmethod pedagogies and ways of enabling learners and teachers to engage with the dynamic, complexity and uncertain nature of intercultural language education in the twenty-first century, there has been limited discussion of such ethical values in the use of intercultural research methods or of decolonizing methodologies in language and intercultural communication. As Holliday notes, such approaches are not readily present in the social scientific methodologies which have dominated the fields of applied linguistics and inter-cultural education over the past decades:

> There is a profound methodological issue here. A non-critical, post-positivist sociology has for too long carried out research which is led by researcher-generated questions in interviews and questionnaires, and has not made room for people who are being researched to express their own agendas. Decentred research methodologies need to allow critical spaces in which the unexpected can emerge, and the narratives of subjects can take on a life of their own (Holliday, 2004/2006, 2007, p. 93). It is perhaps too uncannily obvious that researchers should restrain themselves as far as is possible from imposing their own agendas on what their subjects tell them. (2009, p. 147)

It is my contention in this paper that whilst ethical questions have been brought to bear on theoretical and practical issues of research and of intercultural language pedagogy, there has yet to be a concomitant, creative exploration of decolonizing research methods in the field. In this journal, to take the example to hand, though this is by no means exceptional, papers fall between the theoretical discussion of weighty ethical issues and those driven by data gained and codified according to the normative assumptions of social scientific method. In all of these discussions, where critical questions of language teaching methods and postmethods were in develop-ment, no critical attention was paid to the methods used to gain the data, usually extractive in nature, which supported the work. This raises particular questions for research in the field.

Were such methods decolonizing and restorative in their approach, did they work towards a decentring of the researcher? Did they explore a plurality of literature in other languages and advance suggestions as to how this might be achieved and conform to varying ethical codes of practice at the institutional and international level? Did the research advance approaches which were co-productive, working post-hypothesis rather than to a hypothesis? Were creative methods in play, using narrative, oral history, multimedia, biography, sensory ethnography (Pink, 2009) and doing so according to participatory action research principles (research 'with' not 'on') which would allow marginalized perspectives to be formally setting the agenda for the research? Were aesthetic forms brought in to focus and aesthetic questions posed of the data, the mode of research, the participation? How was the research good, just, beautiful, even, and how were such subjective criteria brought into contact with the value-laden normative demands for linear analysis, codification and systematic presentation of data? I ask these questions as they pertain to important ethical concerns in the posing of research questions, the designing of research, the gathering of research data and the analysis of this data.

The questionnaire, interview or even the ethnographic observation may indeed proceed in an intercultural language field according to the ethical norms for gathering data and may even attempt to work to participatory principles. Surely if intercultural language research is to be truly intercultural in its ethics and aesthetics, it needs to find creative ways for opening up a space where the subaltern cannot just speak (Spivak, 1999) but where the principles of ethical research dialogue can be formed and framed in such ways as to accord space for researcher and researched, subaltern and dominant researcher to create together and to continuously negotiate the meanings and dynamics and the potential for aesthetic resonance of their speech such that the speech and speakerhoods may debate, dialogue, translate, interpret and chorus their understandings and hopes for their particular intercultural world. What are the limits and the possibilities for ethical, genuinely co-created research in systems of higher education and teaching which reward research in performative terms and foster conservative approaches to research methodology through the practice of peer review and citation indices.

Posing such ethical questions of intercultural language research methods is not dissimilar to identifying dual aporias in the universalizing theoretical assumptions of language and intercultural communication or identifying the shifts in learning and teaching methodology in pragmatic terms which have accompanied the societal needs for languages, as Byram and Kumaravadivelu have done in their respective fields during the timeframe under review in this paper (Byram, 1997, 2000, 2008a; Byram & Feng, 2006; Byram & Fleming, 1998; Byram et al., 2001; Kumaravadivelu, 2012b). It does, however, leave the onus on the author to suggest a track for exploring possibilities in methodological terms for the field.

Towards ethical intercultural research methods

My own methods for intercultural research have long developed within the ethical guidance of the Association for Social Anthropology, which is linked to sister organizations worldwide. I have proceeded with increasing belief in participatory, co-productive and co-designed research which reflected my ever widening experience of working in multilingual and intercultural contexts with asylum seekers and refugees. I have subjected my own position to intense scrutiny and usually not liked what I found. It has also taken me into places of considerable ontological risk (Phipps, 2012). The more I have supervised students, the more I have become aware of the gulf between three key poles of research: (i) the normative nature of methods taught (qualitative; interviews as a default for qualitative research) and their compliance with a range of institutional codes all ensuring 'methodological hygiene' – to borrow Deborah Cameron's phrase (1995); (ii) the intercultural subject in all its complexity as colonial, hybrid and decolonizing subject; (iii) the increasingly legalistic frameworks at work in ethics committees and the recourse to laws on data protection and intellectual property, which force and reward normative methodologies – peer review, ethics committees, promotions, funding bodies, research assessment regimes (Strathern, 2000).

What the interactions have produced between these different strictures is often bizarre and to my mind unethical and potentially closes down spaces for genuine co-creative work. It creates a context in which research methods continue to be extractive, often uncritically imposed, and damaging in ways which are entirely avoidable if decolonizing and restorative ethical design is the norm in the critical reflective practice of holistic research design, and if it is recognized as such institutionally. The ethics forms at my own institution are a case in point. I am required to give a date for the destruction of data. I have been working with refugees and we have been sharing common stories of home. These stories are precious to us.

It would be wrong and harmful for me to enact a second destruction of home, for the sake of a tick on a box on a form. The idea, for example, of using an interview schedule or a questionnaire, of plonking a tape recorder on a table, explaining the place of a consent form and asking for a signature, whilst also asking for photographs, enacts bureaucratic procedures well documented by scholars of colonialism (Anderson, 1991; Pratt, 2008), which centre the researcher in a nexus of legislation and protection and which tamper from the outset with the nature of the research relationship and use various strategies to mask the power relations in play. Yet such procedures are now the 'accepted "ethical" norm' in the training of students to undertake research in intercultural settings.

Standardized, extractive methods were not created for complex, postmodern, postcolonial or even simple intercultural situations, but for work under modernist paradigms of knowledge and central control. They too partake of the dual aporias identified by MacDonald and O'Regan (2012) enacting a similar belief in transcendence and a similar belief in the universal value of either qualitative or quantitative approaches to data 'extraction', 'mining'; or to critical theorizing as a responsive solution. In addition, they work along the lines Cryle (op. cit.) identified as 'unproductive', by using methods where awareness raising is both a technique (informed consent) and an end result (changed policy/social impact). This nexus of standard legalistic procedures, assumed methods and aporias leads to a situation where textures of intercultural life are missing. According to Law, these textures include:

> Pains and pleasures, hopes and horrors, intuitions and apprehensions, losses and redemptions, mundanities and visions, angels and demons, things that slip and slide, or appear and disappear, change shape or don't have much form at all, unpredictabilities, these are just some of the phenomena that are hardly caught by social sciences methods. (2004, p. 2)

The situation identified by Tuhiwai Smith (2012), MacDonald and O'Regan (2012), Firth and Wagner (1997, 2007), Cryle (2002) and Young (1996), amongst others is rather bleak and leaves the researcher somewhat hung out to dry, when it comes to developing a practice of intercultural ethics. The theory and critique may be in place, but the complex situation of creative, decolonizing research is compounded by ethical procedures, methods courses in social sciences and extractive approaches to data gathering make it difficult to proceed. It leaves the question open as to what methods might be suggested for decolonizing, ethical intercultural research. Elaborating this fully is clearly beyond the scope of this particular discussion, and marks a new direction in intercultural language scholarship, requiring far more attention than this one paper can achieve. In conclusion, however, I would like to make some initial, tentative suggestions.

Intercultural methods, which we engage to develop and refine intercultural and language pedagogies, need to proceed with a certain naiveté and at one and the same time with a critical commitment to ethical, decolonizing practice. The critical principles of *Language and Intercultural Communication*'s own mission statement mean that a move towards exploring a critical integrity of methodology is long overdue.

The work of Tuhiwai Smith (2012) is exemplary in this regard, articulating an agenda for research which can transcend the imperializing projects of the past and enable redress. She itemizes 25 actions for enabling research with colonized and indigenous peoples which is of real significance to the aims of any truly, holistic and critical study of language and intercultural relations. It draws deeply on legal frameworks which have been hard won but which project the idea of the commons, which challenge simplistic and individual notions of intellectual property. For many indigenous peoples 'research' is a term which has brought near annihilation. Intercultural research – without sustained, careful, collaborative listening and co-construction of its research – risks becoming equally feared and compromised under the normative pressure of research methods conventions. There are ways for us to proceed, worked out collaboratively in the very institutions and organizations most damaged by such methods. Working with those organizations, scholars and communities who have noted their complicity and drawn up guidelines, collaboratively, to support future methodological work. Tuhiwai Smith refers to these as follows:

> In the New Zealand context research ethics for Maori Communities extend far beyond issues of individual consent and confidentiality. In a discussion of what may constitute sound ethical principles for research in Maori communities Ngahuia Te Awekotuku had identified a set of responsibilities which researchers have to Maori people. This framework is based on the code of conduct for the New Zealand Association of Social Anthropologists [. . .]. (2012, p. 119)

Developing a skill in decolonizing research methodologies, which actively works to foster trust, relationship, empathy and co-production with and in languages, and within intercultural relationships, requires, I believe, a fresh approach and a political challenge by critical researchers to the hegemony of dominant social science methodologies. It will mean learning from centres where such research methods have been tested and developed, and from institutions which have examined the nature of the 'occidental gaze' (see Nair-Venugopal, 2012), such as the Institute for Occidental Studies (IKON), Universitii Kebangsaan, Malaysia, host to the first International Association for Languages and Intercultural Communication (IALIC) conference in Asia. It will mean working with humility and an aesthetic openness to different forms. Researchers attempting to work in these ways are not likely to have it easy, given the vested interests of methodological norms, especially in the social and medical sciences. A degree of artistry will be necessary which emerges from encounter and is an outcome of co-design and co-production.

From what Ricoeur terms 'first' naiveté there is the possibility of moving towards 'second naiveté' (1967), where we develop a 'symbolic competence' (Kramsch, 2006); and integrate critical and interpretative elements with a certain artistry or poetics. Symbolic competence allows for openness in interpretation and critical work whilst also making space for others involved in the whole research process to bring their own interpretations to bear.

With this methodological artistry, human beings can accommodate incredulity, conflict or impasse, rather than resolving them one way or another. A naiveté of assumption and a naiveté of direction is in play. Intercultural methods need to be appropriate to the circumstances and context and therefore require initial 'first', credulous naiveté as their opening stance. 'I do not know how you live your life, what you assume, what practices you have learned and evolved, but I assume that you have "named your world"', as Freire terms this (1970, p. 88). Already this differs from the opening stance involved in standard requests (this is one I received recently):

> As part of the research, I'm conducting 'key informant' interviews with people who may have particular insights into the issues and outlooks on account of their experience. If

you are willing to act as a key informant, this would involve being interviewed by me by Skype for 45–60 minutes. The interview will be fairly open.

An open invitation to listen and follow not where the researchers' hypothesis is leading so much as to develop shared views of 'data', shared interpretive strategies, to co-write research and to drop the inappropriate discourse of 'interviews' and 'informants' and 'semi-structured'.

Each research situation is unique and uniquely intercultural as well as uniquely marked linguistically and discursively. It has its own form and processes of embodiment which change through an encounter with others, through habituation and over time (Fabian, 1983; Ingold, 2011). Methods which enable this dynamic to be present and emerge include methods of participatory action research, where questions and problems are co-constructed and address needs present in the field of practice. Whilst there is a risk of implicit transcendence, I believe there is also an untapped scope in restorative methods for intercultural research. Where conflict has occurred or where methods may unwittingly harm, where groups investigated have a certain vulnerability, using methods which have a restorative effect, which can follow trajectories of trauma healing or which may be able to enable repair through representation and creative practice have much to recommend them. This may also be where Aristotlean ethics, connecting ethics to aesthetics (second naiveté, symbols, poetics, artistry) come together, enabling other media or other languages and places to be working, gathering, creating modes which generate new forms for representation.

Oral histories, memory, archiving, collecting and displaying can all contribute to giving renewed and different definition to individual experiences or collective histories. Intercultural research methods which are adept at creating opportunities for such restorative work, and reflecting on the findings have an implicit ethical basis and ability to move beyond situations of pain or conflict. Again, care is needed for such work not to proceed too quickly on trajectories of 'salvation' such as those identified by Abu-Lughod (2002). To these may be added a range of methods from the arts and humanities: creative methods – intercultural 'makings' – art and poetry (Heaney, 1995, 1998; Heidegger, 1971; Phipps & Saunders, 2009), narrative and drama (Baraldi, 2006; Byram & Fleming, 1998; Kohler Riessmann, 2008; Speedy, 2008), legislative theatre and devising all offer scope for engaging methods which are sensory, embodied and which do not simply rely on verbal or textual data gathering in the form of transcripts or questionnaires (Boal, 1998, 2000). These methods have their place, but not in fine-grained intercultural research, and if the prestige of consciousness is to be avoided then methods which rely on the collection of consciousness will also need to be avoided. Narrative inquiry is able to work with a 'breach' and with events, incidents, memories drawing them in to the particular and the universal and opening a space for a different kind of reflection which engages the imagination in artistry. The flattened, coded tones of transcripts, with their numbered rows are divorced from the highly storied, narratively and performatively rich contexts of intercultural communication. If data gathering is to proceed in the ways I sketch above, then there need to be concomitant changes in the modes of its presentation; forms which go beyond the coded transcript, the data table, the quotation and into other media. A fundamental, creative and tentative exploration of different approaches to research is required for this field, such as has emerged in others.

To these methods come those already in use in intercultural research, under the critical sanction of research ethics codes which have been elaborated with indigenous peoples: those of ethnography, participant observation and experiential learning, as documented by Roberts et al. in *Language Learners as Ethnographers* (2001). This strand of research is currently developing in co-productive ways, not just to include autoethnography, but also with visual methods and sensory ethnography (Pink, 2009). These emerge as highly productive ways of collecting, analysing and reflecting on the visceral dimensions of human life which Law calls for in his study of methods in the social sciences (Law, 2004; Law & Mol, 2002). Following de Certeau (1984) and Ingold and Vergunst's work in anthropology (2008), Woitsch demonstrates how productive and compelling such sensory methods can be in her 'intercultural walks' (2011). In this work she invites her language student participants not to an interview, but to take her on a walk and show her significant sights, and to take photographs of the things that have stood out for them as significant. Here we see a method in action which is not based on deficit, does not assume what will be found or judge the items and places, but works in a mode of exploration and embodiment, to allow a flow of action, impressions, natural conversation, showing and relationship. The researcher in Woitsch's work accompanies aspects of intercultural life and allows the form they take to be the form participants chose for representation and in which they are collected: aesthetic, sensory and with performed artistry. The research is quite literally walked. The difference she finds has implications for her own practice and those she researches with, where something lovely is made together which would not have been made without the research practices; something which is restorative and valued beyond an 'interview'. The changed discourse is unsettling – the abandon-ment of words like 'data', 'interview', 'informant', in favour of poetic metaphors of 'walks'; 'footprints', – but it represents an attempt at a decolonizing methodology in intercultural language research.

> Language pedagogy needs emotions, wonder, awe, and magic. These elements are the essence of why people travel and move towards unfamiliar worlds with the help of unfamiliar languages, when their travel is freely chosen and not under duress. Language pedagogy too often leaves this colourful mixture of discovery and learning behind and creates an understanding of language learning as something technical and instrumental, disconnected from 'the world out there'. [. . .] there is more about intercultural language learning than competences, functionalities and outcomes. Instead we may find narratives and experiences in between failure and success with magical as well as highly unsettling touches, which, I argue, are the very essence of what is needed to re-enchant the understanding of intercultural language learning. (Woitsch, 2011, pp. 237–238)

Conclusion

A final note of caution is perhaps required which allows for intercultural practice to continue without risking the paralysis of critique or the fear of harm, or worse, the cultural relativity that misapplied notions of respect can engender in the face of what are identified as cultural habits or norms. There are harmful practices in this world which have the weight of power, prestige, patriarchy and habit behind them, to keep them in place and to force them, often violently, to remain the practices they are. Education can be a source for loosening such habits, as can the arts, as has been repeatedly demonstrated by the education of women worldwide, and the urgency with which this needs to be addressed. It is 'culturally normal' for countries like my own to possess and threaten the use of weapons of mass destruction even though their possession and threatened use violates international law. It is culturally 'normal' to adopt apathy and a belief that nothing will be changed by a small change in practices of, for instance, consumption (a switch to ethical or fair trade, the boycott of certain goods for countries involved in brutal occupation or oppression). It is also common to find scientific 'objectivity' or 'neutrality' as a guise for inactivity and disengagement (Eagleton, 2003).

Intercultural ethics and methods are never 'neutral' or 'objective' as such, and poststructuralism has revealed the fallacy of such assumed positions of neutrality. No method is in and of itself neutral or objective, particularly not a decolonizing one. It is a truism, but not to advocate change where harm is involved is equally a political act. Addressing unjust practices requires both advocacy and as often as not an engagement with the flawed but best institutions we have of law and politics. Intercultural methods and ethics need to be able to apply their findings in these contexts, with poise, subtlety, consideration and artistry, so that students and other actors are well formed in their habits of engagement with civil society and its instruments. This includes engagement with religious instruments and their power to form and control and free, with the law and politics with their ability to carefully and with measured consciousness and balance, to bring the kinds of justice which are the foundation of healing, reconciliation and justice.

This is the territory Gillian Rose claims for philosophy in her difficult but brilliant work, *The Broken Middle* (1992). Writing at the height of postmodernity's quest to free ethics from human institutions of law, civil society, government, family and religion, and to romanticize notions of self, community and freedom, Rose argues not for the 'diremption' – the forcible separation – of law from ethics, but of their muddled togetherness and mutual necessity.

Perhaps, then, intercultural methods can proceed through certain commitments, worked out and articulated by researchers, but open to revision and reflection, as is in the nature of academic dialogue. Maybe there is a danger of a universalizing or a transcendental element creeping in but perhaps there is a greater danger if a purity of political consciousness, or a false adherence to 'neutrality', is sought which eschews artistry or craft. Perhaps it is through 'second naiveté' that intercultural ethics can commit to methods which may enable the seeking of justice and equality in relationships. This would take the field beyond the 'dirtiest of words', research, and towards an embrace of complexity and open-endedness; engagement with what is known or believed to be restorative, collaborative, participatory, sensory, even healing; to allowing for methodological creativity and artistry, which moves towards shaping an intercultural poetics.

Acknowledgements
My thanks to Katja Frimberger for assisting with the German translation.

References
Abu-Lughod, L. (2002). Do Muslim women really need saving? Anthropological reflections on cultural relativism and its others. *American Anthropologist, 104*(3), 783–790.

Adejunmobi, M. (2004). *Vernacular palavar: Imaginations of the local and non-native languages in West Africa.* Clevedon: Multilingual Matters.

Akbari, R. (2008). Postmethod discourse and practice. *TESOL Quarterly, 42*(4), 641–652.

Anderson, B. (1991). *Imagined communities: Reflections on the origin and spread of nationalism.* London: Verso.

Appadurai, A. (1996). *Modernity at large: Cultural dimensions of globalization.* Minneapolis: University of Minnesota Press.

Aristotle. (2002). *Nicomachean ethics.* Newburyport, MA: Focus.

Baraldi, C. (2006). *Education and intercultural narratives in multicultural classrooms.* Rome: Offizina edizioni.

Bauman, Z. (2000). *Liquid modernity.* Oxford: Polity.

Boal, A. (1998). *Legislative theatre: Using performance to make politics.* London: Routledge.

Boal, A. (2000). *Theater of the oppressed.* London: Pluto Press.

Bourdieu, P. (2000). *Pascalian meditations.* Cambridge: Polity.

Byram, M. (1997). *Teaching and assessing intercultural communicative competence.* Clevedon: Multilingual Matters.

Byram, M. (2000). *Routledge encyclopedia of language teaching and learning.* London: Routledge.

Byram, M. (2008a). *From foreign language education to education for intercultural citizenship.* Clevedon: Multilingual Matters.

Byram, M. (2008b). *From foreign language education to education for intercultural citizenship: Essays and reflections.* Bristol: Multilingual Matters.

Byram, M., & Feng, A. (2006). *Living and studying abroad: Research and practice.* Clevedon: Multilingual Matters.

Byram, M., & Fleming, M. (1998). *Language learning in intercultural perspective: Approaches through drama and ethnography.* Cambridge: Cambridge University Press.

Byram, M., Nichols, A., & Stevens, D. (2001). *Developing intercultural communication in practice.* Clevedon: Multilingual Matters.

Byram, M., & Parmenter, L. (2012). *The common European framework of reference: The globalisation of language education policy.* Bristol: Multilingual Matters.

Cameron, D. (1995). *Vergal hygiene.* London: Routledge.

Corbett, J. (2003). *An intercultural approach to English language teaching.* Clevedon: Multilingual Matters.

Corbett, J. (2010). *Intercultural language activities.* Cambridge: Cambridge University Press.

Cormeraie, S., Parry, M., & Killick, D. (2000). *Revolutions in consciousness: Local identities, global concerns in Languages and Intercultural Communication.* Leeds: IALIC.

Crawshaw, R., Callen, B., & Tusting, K. (2001). Attesting the self: Narration and identity change. *Language and Intercultural Communication, 1*(2), 101–119.

Cronin, M. (2000). *Across the lines: Travel, language and translation.* Cork: Cork University Press.

Cronin, M. (2002). 'Thou shalt be one with the birds': Translation, connexity and the new global order. *Language and Intercultural Communication, 2*(2), 86–95.

Cryle, P. (2002). Should we stop worrying about cultural awareness? In S. Cormeraie, D. Killick, & M. Parry (Eds.), *Revolutions in consciousness: Local identities, global concerns in languages and intercultural communication* (pp. 23–34). Leeds: IALIC.

de Certeau, M. (1984). *The practice of everyday life.* Los Angeles: University of California Press.

Dervin, F. (2012). Taking researching with vs researching on seriously: A detour via the intercultural? In W. Midgley, P.A. Danaher, & M. Baguley (Eds.), *The role of participants in education research.* London: Routledge.

Eagleton, T. (2003). *After theory.* London: Penguin.

Fabian, J. (1983). *Time and other: How anthropology makes its object.* New York: Columbia University Press.

Firth, A., & Wagner, J. (1997). On discourse, communication and (some) fundamental concepts in SLA research. *Modern Language Journal, 81*(3), 285–300.

Firth, A., & Wagner, J. (2007). Second/foreign language learning as a social accomplishment: Elaborations on a reconceptualized SLA. *Modern Language Journal, 91*, 800–819.

Freire, P. (1970). *Pedagogy of the oppressed.* London: Penguin.

Giroux, H. (1988). *Teachers as intellectuals.* New York: Bergin & Garvey.

Giroux, H. (1992). *Border crossings: Cultural workers and the politics of education.* London: Routledge.

Guilherme, M., Glaser, E., & Mendez-Garcia, M.d.C. (2010). *The intercultural dynamics of multicultural working.* Bristol: Multilingual Matters.

Heaney, S. (1995). *The redress of poetry: Oxford lectures.* London: Faber and Faber.

Heaney, S. (1998). Crediting poetry: The Nobel Lecture 1995. In *Opened ground* (pp. 446–467). London: Faber and Faber.

Heidegger, M. (1971). *Poetry, language, thought.* New York: Harper Colophon Books.

Holliday, A. (2009). The role of culture in English language education: Key challenges. *Language and Intercultural Communication, 9*(3), 144–155.

Holmes, P. (2011). Managing academic training and research in intercultural communication: Self-reflection tools for self assessing intercultural competence, University of Durham.

Ingold, T. (2011). *Being alive: Essays on movement, knowledge and description.* Abingdon: Routledge.

Ingold, T., & Vergunst, L. (2008). *Ways of walking: Ethnography and practice on foot.* Aldershot: Ashgate.

Jack, G. (2009). A critical perspective on teaching intercultural competence in a management department. In A. Feng, M. Byram, & M. Fleming (Eds.), *Becoming interculturally competent through education and training.* Clevedon: Multilingual Matters.

Jack, G., & Lorbiecki, A. (2003). Asserting possibilities of resistance in the cross-cultural teaching machine: Re-viewing videos of others. In A. Prasad (Ed.), *Postcolonial theory and organizational analysis: A critical engagement* (pp. 213–232). New York: Palgrave.

Killick, D., Parry, M., & Phipps, A. (2001a). *Poetics and praxis of languages and intercultural communication: Volume I.* Glasgow: University of Glasgow French and German Publications.

Killick, D., Parry, M., & Phipps, A. (2001b). *Poetics and praxis of languages and intercultural communication: Volume II.* Glasgow: University of Glasgow French and German Publications.

Kohler Riessmann, C. (2008). *Narrative methods for the human sciences.* London: Sage.

Kramsch, C. (2006). From communicative competence to symbolic competence. *Modern Language Journal, 9,* 249–252.

Kumaravadivelu, B. (2001). Toward a postmethod pedagogy. *TESOL Quarterly, 35*(4), 357–360.

Kumaravadivelu, B. (2006). TESOL methods: Changing tracks, changing trends. *TESOL Quarterly, 40*(1), 59–81.

Kumaravadivelu, B. (2012a). Critical language pedagogy: A postmethod perspective on English language teaching. *World Englishes, 22*(4), 539–550.

Kumaravadivelu, B. (2012b). *Language teacher education for a global society: A modular model for knowing, analyzing, recognizing, doing and seeing.* New York: Routledge.

Law, J. (2004). *After method: Mess in social science research.* London: Routledge.

Law, J., & Mol, A. (2002). *Complexities: Social studies of knowledge practices.* Durham, NC: Duke University Press.

Lund, A., & O'Regan, J. (2010). National occupational standards in intercultural working: Models of theory and assessment. In M. Guilherme (Ed.), *The intercultural dynamics of multicultural working* (pp. 41–58). Bristol: Multilingual Matters.

MacDonald, M., & O'Regan, J.P. (2012, April 4). The ethics of intercultural communication. *Educational Philosophy & Theory.* Advance online publication.

MacDonald, M., O'Regan, J., & Witana, J. (2009). Intercultural competence in the workplace: Issues arising from the development of national occupational standards for intercultural working in the UK. *Journal of Vocational Education and Training, 61*(4), 375–398.

Nair-Venugopal, S. (2009). Interculturalities: Reframing identities in intercultural communication. *Language and Intercultural Communication, 9*(2), 76–90.

Nair-Venugopal, S. (2012). *The gaze of the West and framings of the East.* New York: Palgrave Macmillan.

Ngugi wa Thiong'o. (1986). *Decolonising the mind: The politics of language in African literature.* Kampala: East African Educational.

nic Eoinn, M. (2005). *Trén bhFearann Breac: An Díláithriú Cultúir agus Nualitríocht na Gaeilge.* Dublin: Cois Life.

Nussbaum, M., & Sen, A. (1993). *The quality of life.* Oxford: Clarendon Press.

Parry, M. (2003). Transcultured selves under scrutiny: W(h)ither languages? *Language and Intercultural Communication*, *3*(2), 101–107.

Pennycook, A. (2007). *Global Englishes and transcultural flows*. London: Routledge.

Phipps, A. (2012). Voicing solidarity: Linguistic hospitality and poststructuralism in the real world. *Applied Linguistics*, *33*(5), 582–602.

Phipps, A., & Saunders, L. (2009). The sound of violets: The ethnographic potency of poetry? *Ethnography and Education*, *4*(3), 357–387.

Pink, S. (2009). *Doing sensory ethnography*. London: Sage.

Pratt, M.L. (2008). *Imperial eyes: Travel writing and transculturation* (2nd ed). New York: Routledge.

Ricoeur, P. (1967). *The symbolism of evil*. Boston: Beacon.

Roberts, C., Byram, M., Barro, A., Jordan, S., & Street, B. (2001). *Language learners as ethnographers*. Clevedon: Multilingual Matters.

Rose, G. (1992). *The broken middle*. Oxford: Blackwell.

Speedy, J. (2008). *Narrative inquiry and psychotherapy*. London: Palgrave.

Spivak, G. (1999). Translation as culture. In I. Carrera Suarez, A. Garcia Ferandez, & M.S. Suarez Lafuente (Eds.), *Translating cultures* (pp. 17–30). Hebden Bridge: Dangaroo Press.

Starkey, H. (2007). Language education, identities and citizenship: Developing cosmopolitan perspectives. *Language and Intercultural Communication*, *7*(1), 56–71.

Strathern, M. (2000). *Audit cultures: Anthropological studies in accountability, ethics and the academy*. London: Routledge.

Thurlow, C. (2002). In the eye of the beholder: Representations of 'intercultural' communication among young 'multicultural' teenagers. In S. Cormeraie, D. Killick, & M. Parry (Eds.), *Revolutions in consciousness: Local identities, global concerns in languages and intercultural communication* (pp. 197–208). Leeds: IALIC.

Ting Toomey, S. (1999). *Communicating across cultures*. New York: Guilford Press.

Tuhiwai Smith, L. (2012). *Decolonizing methodologies* (2nd ed). London: Zed Books.

Woitsch, U. (2011). *Walking through the intercultural field. An ethnographic study on intercultural language learning as a spatial-embodied practice*. Glasgow: University of Glasgow.

Young, R. (1996). *Intercultural communication: Pragmatics, genealogy, deconstruction*. Clevedon: Multilingual Matters.

The uses of oral history in Cyprus: ethics, memory and identity

Holger Briel

Department of Communications, University of Nicosia, Nicosia, Cyprus

The paper discusses an Oral History project undertaken from 2009 to 2012 in Cyprus. As Cyprus is a politically volatile and geographically divided country with a Turkish-Cypriot north and a Greek-Cypriot-dominated south, this project attempted to show ways in which the two sides might be able to re-approach each other by claiming a common past. It also attempted to find a common intercultural and ethical language in which individuals were able to talk about their past, and especially about the good times they shared in their daily lives and how these memories might be utilised to build a common future.

Bu makale, Kıbrıs'ta 2009–12 arası yürütülen Sözlü Tarih projesini tartışmaktadır. Kıbrıs, politik olarak tehlikeye açık ve kuzey'de Kıbrıslı Türkler, güney'de de Kıbrıslı Rumlar olmak üzere de coğrafi olarak da bölünmüş bir ülkedir. Bu projenin çabası da ortak bir geçmiş üzerinden iki toplumun birbirne yeniden yaklaşma olasılığının yollarını göstermektir. Proje, ayni zamanda da bu kişilerin geçmişleri hakkında, özellikle de günlük yaşantılarında paylaştıkları güzel zamanlardan bahsederken, ortak bir gelecek yaratılmasında da faydalanılabilecek ortak kültürler-arası ve etik bir dil bulmaya çalışmaktadır.

1. Introduction

For thousands of years, the Eastern Mediterranean has been a contested area. People (s) have moved within it and came from the outside and settled, continuously displacing already established communities and being displaced in turn. This paper is intended to analyse some of the memories associated with more recent unsettlings in the Eastern Mediterranean and more specifically with Cyprus.[1] The data used in the following stem from an Oral History (henceforth OH) project conducted from 2009 to 2012 in Cyprus and partly funded by the European Union. The so-called SHARP project aimed at adding its voice(s) to the cultural conversations taking place across the island by making them public.

All in all, 110 interviews were conducted on both sides of the Green Line, which since 1974 separates the Northern Turkish-Cypriot part from the Southern Greek-Cypriot one. However, trouble between the two communities had been brewing even before Cyprus gained its independence from Britain in 1960 and would still worsen afterwards. Issues of identity, problematic relationships and differing historical accounts would continue to divide the two communities even until today. And while not explicitly discussed here due to space restraints, the overall SHARP project

27

relates to such issues of memory, memorialisation and the search for identity by specifically analysing the production setting and process and the training of interviewers, the interviews themselves and then the collective interpretation of this data via new media means and debriefing events. Interviewees would typically be older members of both communities: Turkish Cypriots in the north and Greek Cypriots in the south. Additionally, a member of the Armenian minority living in Cyprus was also interviewed. A twofold outcome was expected: the sensitising of the young regarding the older generation's experiences, and, secondly, reassuring the old that their memories and inputs are valued by society and making them understand that new media can go a long way in ensuring that their voices are heard.

The paper will begin by looking at the ways in which OH projects have been conceptualised and used in the past in order to give a voice to marginalised groups, and to work through and, sometimes, against official, state-sponsored memories. It will provide a short survey of the usage of (intercultural) OH projects and discuss some of the issues related to them, such as memory, trauma and identity. Moving on to the specific example of Cyprus, it will show that politically instrumentalised stereotypes about the Other are just that and how individual memories narrated by eyewitnesses and other grassroots accounts speak a different language. Of particular interest in the interviews were questions about how individuals from the two Cypriot communities interacted with each other in the events leading up to the 1974 intervention/invasion of the island by Turkish troops and how these events shaped people's lives and attitudes afterwards. Finally, the hope is expressed that these interviews will contribute to individuals' empowerment and their better under-standing of the historic processes which shaped and is continuing to shape their lives and the ethics of sharing an island.

2. Setting the scene: OH, ethics, visuality, identity and memory

The beginnings of OH research, as traced by Abrams (2010), began in the West with the Unemployed Writers Workshop in the 1930s in the USA in which thousands of Americans were interviewed and painted a patchwork picture of their difficult lives at that time. Oral history evolved over time to encompass a composite field with many other disciplines giving it impulses: anthropology, media studies, linguistics, history, ethnography, political studies, psychology and other disciplines. While much of this early work already foreshadowed the activist stance of many OH projects, many of the following interview projects were used for statistical analysis by governments and academics. It took until the 1960s for OH counter-culture projects to sprout in increasing numbers. The treasure waiting for researchers involved in such projects is aptly described by eminent OH practitioner Passerine:

> Above all, we should not ignore that the raw material of oral history consists not just of factual statements, but is pre-eminently an expression and representation of culture, and therefore includes not only literal narrations but also the dimensions of memory, ideology and subconscious desires. (1979, p. 84)

People began realising that counter-memories were needed in order to complement and challenge official historic discourse and preserve ageing voices. Around the same time, one of the main reservations of historians against OH began to crumble: the charge that OH is overly reliant on unreliable memories and intentions of informers.

The argument was in fact reversed and OH was thought to 'emphasise the truth of the telling versus the telling of the truth' (Frank, 1995, p. 145), while nevertheless adhering to the 'referential pact' existing between historic facts and the re-telling of them by a respondent (Abrams, 2010, p. 47ff, cf. also Meyerhoff, 1992, on memory and retelling history). It was consequently part of a larger movement to take back memory and media from official and oftentimes political authorities. Referring to community radio in India, but also addressing OH issues, Saeed states the following regarding the power of such moves:

> Given the centrality of communication to society, who 'owns' the media, who gets to speak on behalf of whom, and to what end are critical issues. The regression of 'mainstream' media from 'watchdogs' of democracies to business ventures resulting in Habermasian 'refeudalisation of the public sphere' is worrying. Community media re-engage communities on the periphery, opening possibilities for social change. The dominance of mainstream players in media governance, complicated by sustainability concerns of grassroots enterprises, result in legislation that impedes the potentiality of community media access and community radio struggle in India. (2009, p. 466)

This is certainly also true for OH on a global scale. Moreover, by its very nature, it is always already a political act: 'Oral History is a constantly evolving practice that sits at the interface between the personal and the social, between past and present [...]' (Abrams, 2010, p. 174). And today, with further differentiation within the field having taken place, the wish to give a voice to interviewees has evolved into seeing OH 'as a means by which the subjects might empower themselves is not terms of ambition but context' (ibid.). Typically, much OH today is performed via community projects, with contemporary technology allowing for easy access and storage.

There exist certain aspects within OH which might be called its backbone. These are today the considerations of ethics, the visual interview process, questions of identity and memorialisation. All of these impinge on OH and need to be considered in its projects. The first three will be discussed in more theoretical terms in the following, while the latter will be analysed directly in relation to the Cyprus data.

2.1. The ethics of OH

When looking at OH projects, ethics is one of the most important areas of inquiry. It plays an important part in any OH project for the following reasons: these begin with the belief of the investigators that this project will contribute to the further pacification of an area/a country/a region by providing tools for reconciliation work. As has been demonstrated elsewhere (Nuttall & Coetzee, 1998), similar projects were employed by the Reconciliation and Truth Commission in South Africa and Burundi, allowing for the hearing of different voices, making them available to the public and contributing towards a climate of understanding. Ethics is also implicated in the approach of the interviewer. According to Philippe Denis (2007), four major principles of ethics ought to play out in OH: autonomy and respect for the dignity of persons; non-maleficence; beneficence and justice. While he uses these to refer mainly to the relationship between the interviewer and interviewee, I see the role of ethics extending beyond this relationship; encompassing the setting up of interviews, the choice of both interviewers and interviewees, questionnaire/interview design and post-interviews, and analysis and dissemination.

Ethics would also affect one of the main dilemmas of OH research – questions of truth versus securing 'a good' interview. Personal rapport between the interviewer and interviewee has always been a decisive factor in the success of OH research and informs the cooperative aspect of the interview. Frisch goes so far as to speak of the 'shared authority' an OH narrative contains, squarely putting the responsibility for the emerging text on both, the interviewer and the interviewee (1989).[2]

Perhaps not surprisingly, many of the above theoretical considerations have been gleaned from work done in post-apartheid South Africa, for instance, that of the 'Truth and Reconciliation' provenience. In actuality, many of the hearings conducted within the remit of this committee could be framed as OH interviews within a certain institutional framework. Much of this was intercultural in nature, with many ethnicities taking part. And much of it was very painful. In 2012, Sean Field for instance compared the displacement of people in the Cape Town area during apartheid to amputations (2012, p. 2), a physical removal of a body part, accompanied by massive trauma. Such trauma and psychological scarring would also exist in people who have been traumatised by events in the past and who might benefit from participating in interviews and thus working through such events. In effect, this is one of the main reasons for doing OH projects.

Another reason for doing such interviews is the fact that, while there exist UNESCO heritage sites for monuments, and by now even for documentary heritage (Volk, 2008), such venues do not yet exist for OH. OH is still fractured and localised. The sites available on the Internet are mostly individual or small project sites and only sites such as that of the US Oral History Association[3] promise at least some online interlinking. No doubt, in the future, the network structure inherent in the World Wide Web will have its effect also on OH as more and more archives will open up to the public. Moreover, it will be up to these sites to keep alive the memory of people, their diasporic experiences and attempts at dealing with them, oftentimes challenging official histories.

2.2. The new-found visuality of OH

Another important area of change is the interview itself, with visual tools now dominating the documentation process. This is still a relatively new development, especially when it comes to online data storage of such interviews. For example, the broader framework within which the OH project in Cyprus was conducted was the SHARP project[4] and involved enhancing local empowerment through the usage of new media, especially video. The availability of video technology has given yet another dimension to OH projects, and unless there is good reason to speak against the use of video (for reasons of anonymity, for instance), video should play an integral part in OH projects (cf. Baldwin & Lopez, 1990; Bamford, 2011; Giorgis et al., 1999; Stokes, 2001). Video footage becomes yet another mosaic piece in the visual tapestry being woven today due to the ubiquitous availability of video technology. Due to the relative ease with which online archives can be created today, this opportunity is open to more and more individuals interested in undertaking such projects. In addition, there exists good reason for making this effort, given the potential audiences for such work (cf. Sinatra, 1986; Wileman, 1993). Wherever we look today, (moving) images confront us. And increasingly, we express ourselves through (moving) images as well, such as emoticons, profiled pictures or *YouTube* video productions. Ever since Marshall

McLuhan articulated it, we have known that the medium is the message and today's media of choice clearly carry a visual bias. This ubiquity of the image also means that we have to make sense of many more visual cues than in the past. One of the main labours of the twenty-first century therefore is not to hone our skills in interacting with visual media, but also to prepare the next generations of media activists and students for these new media developments.

Especially in communication, the primacy of this sense has traditionally been challenged by other ways of comprehending semiotic processes, most notably by the techniques of literacy, but many of our impulses still remain intrinsically wired to vision. Classic research has suggested that many of our decision processes based on visual stimulation actually precede the conscious reception of the images and thus require even further study (Baldwin & Lopez, 1990; Merikle & Daneman, 1998).

This has been a bane and an advantage. The bane is that we do not use as much of our brainpower in deconstructing such images as it requires, because oftentimes it is believed that images are globally understood and thus do not need translation, unlike writing for instance, which does. The advantage is that with the arrival of help via digital media, we are able to visually encode and decode our worlds in many new ways not available to previous generations.

In order to understand these worlds of global media representations, via media it has become possible to collaborate much more easily and create a social impact. The Arab Spring of 2011 is a very good example of how the power of digital collaborative media can change political realities (Briel, 2008). Therefore, understanding these new and ever more quickly created media worlds has to become a central plank in any attempt to understand society. While new media have the ability to dazzle us, this can only be part of their function. According to data collated by the World Internet Project in 2009, oftentimes through OH projects, it is not so much a question of access to Internet resources any more, but rather of which materials are accessed. Data from Cyprus for instance suggest that there is a correlation between the quality of the web pages students access and their success at school.[5]

The remarkable democratisation of the media sphere enacted via participatory and ubiquitous media has set the stage for today's developments in OH. Here, it is really the smaller projects, initiated by individuals or smaller research consortia, which have come to the fore during this latest media revolution. This is a direct result of the democratisation of digital media production tools over the last 10 years or so. This has allowed not only for the sound bites individuals have been able to insert into the official discourse via OH, but also for something one might call 'VisionBytes' – the ability to globally record, store and disseminate visual material in real time. This is a pivotal turning point in the history of media and social interaction and carries with it the potential to question and challenge existing hierarchies and institutions. Moreover, it is for this reason that the training of individuals in these new media has taken on added urgency and will eventually decide on how successfully we can interact within our social circles and negotiate with those outside of them.

Mediated visual processes have joined the arsenal of tools with which we interpret and create the world. They have become an important device in the fight for social justice and can be a powerful local grassroots apparatus in combating inequality and social digital exclusion. Therefore, they *should* and *could* be improved and developed in educational and training environments, as was the case in the Cypriot OH project.

However, even with these new tools in place, certain areas such as different cultural settings still continue to be in need of consideration.

2.3. OH and identity

Especially when working in different cultures, it is important to remember that their members might react differently to OH situations. It is of importance that interviewers respond as much as possible to respondents' concerns. These might stem from a variety of sources. They could be of a political nature, in that the political situation would not allow for a public display of what the respondent is saying; they might also be of more cultural concerns. After all, at the heart of ethnography and anthropology lies the searching and documenting of cultural differences. In addition, formalised communication situations such as interviews might be considered a strange practice in some cultures. This might require different tactics on the part of the interviewer; these might range from anonymity for the respondent to using different recording devices, for instance, not using video but rather audio only methods. As mentioned above, it is important to remember that the interviewer him/herself also plays an important part. Thus, an interview conducted by a woman might elicit a different response than that by a man. Lastly, a 'confessional' culture as it exists in the West, that is, the willingness to entrust somebody else with one's memories, might not exist in the same way elsewhere, and researchers might have a harder time finding interviewees and also conducting actual interviews.[6]

Typically, in an interview, a respondent actively fashions his/her identity and performs it. S/he will attempt to achieve composure, and only in extreme circumstances might this break down, for instance, when a respondent begins to cry or is unwilling/unable to continue the interview. In other cases, composure will not allow a possible prospective respondent to agree to an interview. There might be several reasons for that. In my experience, this is a common occurrence. Thus, while approaching individuals for the project described here, I was told by one prospective interviewee that he had agreed to being interviewed in the past but that his words had been misconstrued afterwards and that he would unfortunately now have to forego the interview. In another instance, a person declined to participate because she felt she had 'nothing to contribute to the discussion', a statement which was clearly untrue as she is a prominent figure and activist in the local arts and entertainment scene.

Within interviews with participants (including interviewers and interviewees) hailing from different cultural backgrounds, intertextuality is bound to be linguistically present, be it consciously or unconsciously. This is certainly also true for the narrative created, which itself might have preconscious roots. In order to highlight the precarious relationships between individuals from different cultures, or, indeed between interviewer and interviewee in culturally and politically diverse settings, Shanta Nair-Venugopal has coined the term 'interculturalities' (2009, p. 76) for identities that are socially constructed through communicative and discursive practices, and/or mediated through technologies such as the Internet and other media, for instance, the video recorder in the case of OH work, as multimodal constructions of language use. This is a helpful construct for OH practitioners, as many of the projects are concerned with international life stories, especially those in which video techniques are used that allow for non-linguistics components such as gestures and body presence to come to the fore.

3. Cyprus and the OH project[7]

Contemporary Cypriot society is beset by what the Cypriot writer and artist Alev Adil claimed, is a 'secret archive of inherited amnesia'.[8] In many ways, the traumatic experiences of the 1950s, 1960s and 1970s have left deep traces in the local society or societies, depending on what kind of concept about the local one applies.

The political contestations evident in Cyprus are oftentimes related to public memory, the one fed by memorial days and memorials. However, political contestations are of course not only relegated to memories; far from it. For instance, the violence of their military counterparts impacts on human lives in the Middle East and South Eastern Europe every day. However, there are also other, more subtle ways in which such contestations are politicised. An important field is archaeology. In 1998, Lynne Meskell's edited volume, *Archaeology under Fire*, evidences how architecture was used by historic potentates to display their political triumphs. However, the book also describes how architectural history was refashioned by later and present-day governments to influence the way in which certain historic events ought to be viewed, thereby privileging political goals for the creation and dissemination of these memories set in stone. But this memorialisation as reality did not stop with architecture; more than a decade before Meskell's book, Benedict Anderson had already demonstrated in his *Imagined Communities* (2006) how cartography, another way of appropriating territory and history, had been used by the British to create a Thai empire and thus determine political and historical ideologies for decades to come.

Much of this memorialisation in many fields is done through creative cultural venues. In addition, they are also available in abundance in this part of the world.[9] Thus, Ari Folman's compelling and forceful animated feature, *Waltzing with Bashir* (2008), speaks of the horrors and memories aroused by the Israeli occupation of Beirut; and in her short prose, such as *Ledra Street* (2006), and in her poetry, the Armenian-Cypriot writer Nora Nadjarian attests to these fractured memories of the Armenian diaspora. As she claims, memories[10] are not an amorphous mass, they are not experienced equally by their subjects and always represent what has been called 'inherited labour' (Stoler, 2006, p. 283). Collective public memories stem from and are perpetuated by mass media events, for example, the screening of parliamentary debates or sports events and the manifold reprinting of history creating photographs. Opposite these collective ones, there are the private memories. As one project in London clearly states, memories are an asset and must be treated as such.[11] According to Kovacs (2006), there exists a chiastic relationship between the politics of history and personal memory: the *politics of history* is a source of political legitimisation. It is the attempt to justify political goals via 'historical' narratives, whereas personal memory engenders personal identity and seeks to harmonise it with social identities. Both of them merge in a *social* or *collective*. The role of the personal account is to mediate between individual memories and social realities. Kovacs proposes the method of *histoire croisée*, of a writing of history that criss-crosses between these memories and analyses them, focusing on the crossovers of different cultures, social groups and historical events. In OH projects, these two kinds of memories are almost always entwined and inform each other, thus providing a rich field for memory research.[12]

Furthermore, there are oftentimes pressing reasons for the creation of such projects. OH projects are oftentimes called 'living memory' projects, as they attempt to preserve eyewitness accounts. In Cyprus, many people who witnessed or remember the war and (forced) border crossings are getting older and might not have many other chances of getting their voices heard. Research has shown that in many ways older people are disenfranchised by society's ageism and the interviews might go a long way in bolstering the self-image of the respondents and allow them to get their voices recorded as well. As the current generation is getting older and thinning out, these interviews might be the first and last opportunity for the older individuals to tell their side of the story.

And while this particular strand of OH projects might be said to have started with the Shoah Survivor Project at Yale University, the Fortunoff Video Archive,[13] and many others, and closer to the region at hand, have followed suit. For example, the 1998 small project at McNeese State University, entitled *The Mediterranean Oral History Project*,[14] collected interviews with South-west Louisiana residents who emigrated from the Mediterranean region. Also, the EU initiative *Mediterranean Voices: Oral History and Cultural Practice in Mediterranean Cities* (2002–2005)[15] examined the culture of 11 Mediterranean cities, incorporating audio, video and text files.

Additionally, a number of important academic projects and conferences have begun focusing on these issues.[16] Also, between 2003 and 2004, the two-part documentary film entitled *Parallel Trips* by fellow Cypriot directors Panikos Chrysanthou and Derwis Zaim, produced to critical acclaim, was aimed at giving survivors of the 1974 invasion of Cyprus a voice. It addressed issues of the interconnectedness of these memories and processes of remembering and how they are mobilised as symbolic resources in political manoeuvres (cf. Briel, 2008; Scott, 2002).

The present project is part of a number of such projects being carried out in Cyprus at the time of this writing. Other projects are *The Cyprus Oral History Project* (Nikoletta Christodoulou and Lucy Avraamidou), *The Life Stories Project* (Olga Demetriou and Rebecca Bryant) and the *Cyprus 2015* project (Ahmed Sözen). At the time of writing for this issue, all of them were in their last stages and are slated to go officially online within the following months. Thus, issues of reconciliation through remembrance, of official versus unofficial histories, the imagining of homelands, senses of belonging, fractures of struggle or 'Memory, Truth, and the Journey towards a New Past' (Catia Galatariotou) have all found a way into the public discourse and are eliciting information from important cross-border memories.

Moreover, what is becoming evident through these projects is that such memories are not confined to a certain region only. Especially in a shrinking world, these memories continue to traverse the globe, intersecting in many places, mingling with other local memories, and sometimes returning with much cross-fertilised thought (cf. Briel, 2008). Cyprus is no exception. All interviewees have had experiences abroad, in the UK, in the USA, in Turkey and a host of other countries, sometimes willingly, sometimes involuntarily due to the political processes taking place. This ex-territorialisation might actually have allowed them to take a more disaffected viewpoint from others who have never left the island and reach different conclusions.

In terms of practicalities, the interviews conducted for the project had several interviewers. These were mostly MA students from the University of Nicosia's MA in Media and Communication who received training on questionnaire design, camera work, interviewing techniques and post-production. All of them were given free reign to find their interviewees and all of them were rather successful, with many of them easily finding two or three within the space of a few days. However, it was felt that the training would allow the interviewers to get a better grasp of what they were attempting to do and to sensitise them to the technological as well as the human factors involved. Feedback showed that this information was appreciated, but that some of them also just set out to 'do their own thing', overwhelmingly with positive results. Some of the interviews were shot with a professional camera, others with a camera-equipped telephone, still others with a cheap home camera. This diversity was intended. As part of the remit of the European Grant funding, the project was to allow non-specialists to experiment with new media and their use in social research.

The three interviews selected and discussed below were conducted in the autumn of 2011 by one interviewer (the author) and a cameraman as pilots to be shared with the other interviewers. Interviewed were George, a middle-aged Greek-Cypriot media worker, Ali, a retired Turkish-Cypriot contractor and now a second-hand bookshop owner, and Nora, an Armenian-Cypriot writer and educator. The interviewer and the cameraman were non-Cypriots; the interviewer was of German origin and the cameraman of a Serbian background. As discussed in many ethnographic texts, the relationship between 'foreign' interviewers and local respondents is always fraught with difficulty.[17] At the same time, the foreignness of the researcher might also allow for answers not readily provided to other locals. Other project interviews were conducted by Greek and Turkish Cypriots, sometimes in English, sometimes in Turkish. Most of the interviews with Greek Cypriots were, in fact, conducted in English, as were the interviews discussed below. Interestingly enough, English was none of the participants' native language. In addition, these were the first or pilot interviews conducted for the OH project, and this explains why there were still sometimes awkward moments when the interviewer did not know exactly how to respond to an interviewer situation.

3.1. The first interview: George

George is a seasoned Cypriot media worker in his early 50s. He grew up in Cyprus and then moved to the UK and the USA for study and work. He returned to Cyprus to work in the industry and has film production and director credits to his name. Among the films he has directed is one which deals with the Cyprus crisis and the events of 1974. Right from the beginning of the interview, it became clear that he has an easy rapport with the camera, having worked in front of and behind the camera for many years. Judging by his gestures and occasional frowns, he seemed a bit tired, if not wary at first, but this turned into concentrated and willing collaboration with the interviewer. Indeed, one has the impression that he is relieved to tell his story (once again).

He begins his story with life in the early 1970s but then very quickly moves on to the traumatic events of 1974. He recounts at length his childhood memories of the war and of hearing enemy airplanes passing above. After the end of the war, the airport in Nicosia was closed for civil aviation and nowadays it is very rare to hear an airplane crossing the sky over Nicosia. George states that he had forgotten this until he went to London and for the first time in a long while was confronted by airplane noise. His statement is an ample reminder that specific memories (autobiographical/ traumatic) consist of both psychical and social elements, which are oftentimes combined, as in this case.

In his answers, George dispels the myth that all the people were mostly afraid of the 'Turks'. For him the fear of EOKA B, a Greek-Cypriot paramilitary shaped after EOKA A, which had fought the British in the Cypriot anti-colonial struggle, and which now exacted strikes against Turkish Cypriots, was the scarier enemy. However, he also acknowledged that the belligerent events of 1974 had changed his life and that many use these tragic events to their own devices, oftentimes creating (ideological) barriers to innovation and social progress in society. He exemplifies this attitude when he tells the story of his return to Cyprus in the 1980s working for CNN World Report. At one point, he had wanted to cover another item, the breaking AIDS crisis. However, he was asked, 'Why do you want to cover this? We have the Cyprus problem which needs solving first!'

When responding to the last interview question about changes taking place in Cyprus for some kind of re-unification of the two halves, George was seen and heard to be letting out a long and deep sigh, which might be interpreted in two ways: (a) as a sign of resignation or (b) a sign that not everything is lost, but that in Cyprus, things take longer than in other parts of the world.

3.2. The second interview: Ali

Ali, an amicable Turkish Cypriot in his early 70s, is a shop owner in the beautifully restored Büyük Han Market in the Turkish northern part of Nicosia. He has had many professions in his life – he worked as a carpenter and in construction, is a collector of books and stamps and a sportsman. After his retirement, he opened a second-hand book and curiosity store in Büyük Han. He is active in the community and whenever one walks by his shop, one can see many people inside it enjoying his hospitality.

It is clear from the start that, just like George, Ali is also comfortable in front of the camera. He jokes and laughs a lot and is clearly enjoying himself. He proudly mentions that he has been interviewed by foreigners many times over and relishes the memories. Very early on in the interview, Ali comments on the fact that he is fluent in English, Turkish and Greek and thus speaks all three of the island's languages. This allows him to position himself as an expert not just on his own Turkish-Cypriot ethnic background, but also as an interlocutor for the two other official languages of the island.

He grew up in Limassol but moved to Istanbul when he was 19 and then to Kyrenia (Greek: Κερύνεια, Turkish: Girne) and Nicosia after his retirement. His father and mother had remained in Limassol and then 'moved' to Kyrenia. This was directly after the 1974 war and their move was enforced patriation (from Greek 'territory' to Turkish 'territory'). It is not surprising Ali says 'moved', as this is one of his ways of coping with the difficult political situation in Cyprus. He is also keen to stress that he had good relations with the Greek community. 'If I want to buy something [at a house/shop], I was invited to the house.' This in his eyes was a sign of inclusion in the Greek community. Prodded to tell one of his stories from the old days, he responds: 'Every day is history', insinuating that for him the small events count as much as the big ones. And indeed he does not tell a story until the close of the interview; the story of a burglary at his house (in Istanbul, not in Cyprus!), which prompted him to stay away from it for a whole week. Psychologically, this might be explained as a belated reaction to the Cyprus events (the forced removal of his parents and the loss of their family home) and his replaced fear. Just as he was away from Cyprus during some of the unrest, thus avoiding major calamities for himself, he now stays away from his house longer than objectively necessary in order not be exposed to a perceived risk.

Apart from being a gifted narrator and performer, Ali is also a master of evasion. Asked whether he sees the 'old days' of both communities living together peacefully returning again, he replies: 'This is a political question. I keep away from that. ... I am a very good mathematician and am also good at hunting.' A little later he comes back to the subject, though: 'We pay politicians to do things for us. That's it. We do not need to be involved. A normal life is better.' This statement speaks very clearly about his politics, at least when talking to us. He stays away from it, even implying that politics is 'un-normal'. He also stresses the use of the word 'happy' when referring to himself, which appears time and again. And, lastly, he stresses that 'if you have so many problems in the past, you work on your body'. Besides that, according to his statements, you also withdraw further into your private matters. Throughout the interview, Ali put great emphasis on his hobbies: 'I judge international stamps. I have been in exhibitions. I am also a chess player ...' He is proud of his body and mentions that he has been a runner and still goes walking in Troodos, the highest mountain range and spanning both parts of Cyprus. This last bit of information is again a hint that he does not see Cyprus as a divided entity.

3.3. *The third interview: Nora*

The third interviewee, Nora, exemplifies the fact that the political and violent episodes in recent Cyprus history not only affected Greek Cypriots as the majority of inhabitants on the island, Turkish Cypriots as the largest minority on the island, but also other minorities, such as Armenians and the Maronites.

Nora is a teacher in her 40s at the Armenian School in Nicosia and also a prolific writer of poetry and shorter prose. She asked to be interviewed at home where she 'feels comfortable'. Just like the other two interviewees, it is clear that she is relaxed in speaking to the camera. Being a teacher and celebrated artist, she is used to explaining things in public and giving her opinion. She is composed and keen to tell her side of the story. She begins by telling the interviewer that there are 3000–3500 Armenians still living on Cyprus and that they have always been active in the arts, culture and music of both communities. She is obviously proud of her heritage, but also emphasises that 'the Armenian diaspora has always integrated well ... Armenians are not foreigners, but separate'.

Nora recalls her childhood in Limassol and especially a cat which also features in one of her short stories, *Ledra Street*. In the beginning of the interview, and especially when referring to her childhood, her eyes sparkle and she laughs and smiles a lot, so much so that at one point she asks for a minute to regain her composure. This light-heartedness would give way to a more earnest expression when talk about the events of 1963 and 1974 begins.

She recalls the day the sirens went off and her childhood ended, using words such as 'bittersweet' and 'traumatic'. Like the other interviewees, she reiterates the stories told by her parents and grandparents about how good life was in the old days, that is, before 1963, when all communities lived together peacefully. Significantly, it was her mother who talked about the old days while her father did not dwell on them at all. Moreover, just like George, who first had to go abroad to meet a Turkish Cypriot, she said that she did not meet one until 1974.

Nora also declared that she only realised that she was living on a divided island when she moved away from Limassol (which was by the seaside and far from the Green Line dividing the two communities) to Nicosia, the divided capital which sits on the Green Line. And it was this event, the first-hand experience of division which set her off on her writing career, looking back at what she had lost and assessing the present. Moreover, she alleges, such a move does not work if you write about barbed wire and borders, but rather, one needs to have them reflected and embedded in the emotions of the characters described. She thereby hopes to capture those times and by having people reflect on what has been happening hopes they might possibly change their attitudes for the better. She joyfully recounts one of her readings in New Zealand and how she had the impression that her stories really moved people.

4. Analysis of the interviews

When analysing the interviews, it becomes clear that all three individuals interviewed seemed to enjoy the telling of their stories. They are experienced narrators and have many elements of their stories readily available. They view the telling as empowerment and also as a bridge between their professional and private selves.

Significantly, all three stress that the old days were better, a sentiment shared by the majority of the people interviewed. This might have several reasons. For one, this is a mindset oftentimes found among older people and since all interviewed were older than 50 years, most of them significantly so, this might be the general sentiment that has appeared time and again. For another, this age group still remembers the 'old days' and are aware of the fact that a common, shared life had been possible for both communities before, whereas this is not the case for the younger generation.

While generally, much banter and goodwill was displayed and visible in the interviews, however, when it came to the individual events of the early 1960s and in 1974, the mood changed, at least for George and Nora. And this is not surprising, given the nature of the events discussed. This also implies that when doing research on events which might have induced trauma in respondents, special care needs to be taken. Studies on Holocaust survivors have proven that traumatic experiences are hard to relate, as they have had a profound effect on the respondent. And Ali would be included here, as his refusal to acknowledge any of these issues is in itself an attempt to keep these events at bay. Different respondents react differently to the re-telling of a trauma-inducing event. Some might go quiet, whereas others use the interview to cathartic effect in that pain is extraterritorialised (Dawson, Rogers, & Leydesdorff, 1999). In our sample the respondents acted in very different ways: George told a story about his fear of hearing airplanes due to his experiences in the 1974 war, whereas Ali refused to recall any traumatic experiences. Nora has tried to work through the events by becoming a writer. In George's and Nora's case, this re-telling might have a cathartic effect to help overcome any trauma by cladding the experience into a stock narrative and thus making it a manageable part of one's self history. In Ali's case, any trauma associated with the events was downplayed and evaded, which is another way of managing it.

For all interviewees, one might apply the theory of compartmentalisation of events into several modes. Portelli (1997, pp. 24–27) stipulates that OH narratives generally adopt three different modes: the institutional, the communal and the personal. In OH narratives, each one of these is characterised by the usage of a different personal pronoun: the third person singular for the institutional, the first person plural 'we' for the communal and the first person singular 'I' for the personal. In our sample, all three modes appear, although the personal memory dominates in two accounts, suggesting that agency is at a prime for both these interviewees, but an agency which is mostly reduced to personal and less to institutionalised interactions.

Due to the perceived evasion strategies employed especially by the second respondent, both interviewer and cameraman experienced a certain kind of frustration, as they had had other topics in mind. All three interviewees used emplotment strategies in which they presented themselves to the interviewer in a certain light (the politically interested media professional, the generally happy apolitical retiree and the writer trying to make fictionalised sense of events) and by refusing to discuss certain topics. This might be stated outright or with the use of certain words (e.g. 'troubles' rather than the more appropriate 'deadly raids' or 'war' for the unrests in the 1960s and the Turkish intervention/invasion of 1974). The interviews can thus also be read as an exercise in narrativity and how to structure modern-day narratives within contested and intercultural social settings and offer personal solutions on social challenges. In this sense they are also literary undertakings, but 'literary' applied in a broad sense, and more and more inclusive of and dependent on new media and technology.

It should go without saying that sometimes interviews do not go according to plan. In the case of the Ali interview, even the cameraman intervened twice and proposed clarifications for the questions posed. However, this was more of a problem for the interviewers than for the respondent and rightly so. Oftentimes, for the success of an OH interview it is important that the respondent has the feeling that s/he is in a position of power and can speak from this position. And despite the frustration felt by an interviewer, the outcome of such an interview might actually be quite good, as different strategies such as not talking about certain events can be observed and analysed as easily as ones in which issues are discussed outright (cf. Stoler, 2006).

All three respondents were content with being interviewed at their respective places of work, George in his office, Ali in his shop and Nora at home where she spends much of her time writing. George was able to tell a story right away, perhaps also because the airplane story was one he had recounted numerous times. Ali had so many stories that it was hard for him to concentrate on any one in particular. And Nora had written down many of her stories, but was willing to give insights into their creation process. It is remarkable that all three of them were not keen to speak directly about politics, with George being more open than Ali or Nora. George stressed the fact that he did not leave Cyprus permanently, because for him it was worth fighting for a solution on the island itself and thus stay true to his roots. Ali did not explain why he moved back to Cyprus following his retirement, but his life on the island is ample proof that he considers it his home. However, Ali refrains from speaking about politics and sees his own body rather than the country of his residence as a construction site. In all three cases, the interviews revealed how much the Cyprus problem has intervened in their lives and altered their life choices and attitudes. All three of them made their choices accordingly: George came back to

Cyprus and entered the media field to perhaps affect some changes in the thinking of the population in the south; Ali came back restricting himself to his own body and the book and tourism trade; Nora began her writing career. It is fair to say that without the events of 1974, their lives would have moved on different tracks but they have found coping mechanisms and coherence systems to deal with the ensuing changes: George and Nora in a more professional capacity, Ali in a more private one. In all three, composure appears to have been achieved through the re-telling of their stories, be it politically, apolitically or artistically.

5. Conclusion

The series of interviews undertaken aimed at providing an up-to-date snapshot of Cypriots and the interviewees' views on the past and its relevance for the present. From the three interviews discussed above, it became clear that all three individuals were and still are affected by the events of the 1960s and 1970s and that while individual composure has been achieved, closure on the other hand, individually, communally or bi-communally, has not. The remaining interviews speak to the same fact: all respondents agree that the status quo is untenable (unless one, like Ali, uses most of one's intellectual defences to expunge politics) and in need of change. The interviewers became better able to appreciate the fraught process of reconciliation when they were introduced to individualised life stories (Frank, 1995; Linde, 1983), not only from their own community but from the 'others' as well, thus creating another perspective from the official records on both sides and a more ethical one.

The interviews conducted during this project made it clear that much of the Cypriot memory and identity research work is still going on. All respondents were trying to make sense of their own identity vis-à-vis the general political situation in returning to individualised events in their pasts. As there are other ongoing projects scattered across the island, OH has of recent times, become an important tool in working through memories and collecting them. The next task will be to provide a more centralised way of accessing all these diverse interviews and thus making it easier for future researchers to access this much needed material. It is important to involve the next generations, as they will become the guardians of this knowledge and should be given as many narrations as possible to evaluate. Due to the technology available today, especially video equipment and easy storage facilities, this job is becoming easier as time goes by. Yet, training, motivational discourse and institutional support are all still required in order to get projects such as the current ones off the ground, a task the EU, UN and national governmental and non-governmental institutions all need to work on together in order to provide the basis for success.

Notes

1. The description of the full project can be found at http://www.sharpnetwork.eu
2. This shared authority is of course already well known in cultural production. One might think of the *Ècriture automatique* that Dada employed, that is, the blind co-creating of a text with others; various initiatives in Eastern bloc countries, such as the Bitterfelder Weg in the East Germany of the early 1960s, where industrial workers were asked to collaborate on the writing of literature, or, closer to home, digital literature projects or, indeed, collaborative blogging (cf. for the latter Briel, 2012). All of these projects have the

following in common: a narrative is co-created, disseminated and received by a hybrid audience. This is certainly also the case for OH projects.

3. www.oralhistory.org
4. http://wwwsharpnetwork.eu
5. http://www.worldinternetproject.net/_files/_Published/_oldis/CyprusWIPsemiFINAL. pdf
6. Thus, in the Philippines, stories of selfhood as such do not exist as much as in the West and individual accounts oftentimes privilege community over individual. Cf. Abrams (2010, p. 33).
7. The interviews can be accessed at: http://www.sharpnetwork.eu
8. Alev Adil, performing on 5 March 2012 at ARTos Foundation, Nicosia.
9. For a discussion on this for the region, cf. Briel (2008), Brown (2003), Butler (2009), Canefe (2007), Leventis (2002), Leventis, Murata, and Hazama (2008), Makdidi (2006), Papadakis (2005, 2006), Scott (2002) and Troebst (2001).
10. Recently, much has been written on memory and its relationship to identity and history in the region. The reader might want to consider the following: Canefe (2006), Goody (2007), Hamilton and Shopes (2008), Haugbolle (2005), Hodgkin and Radstone (2003), Kaufman (2004), Makdidi (2006), Öztürkmen (2006), Sa'di and Abu-Lughod (2007), and Schacter (1996).
11. The Memory Bank: http://www.thememorybank.co.uk
12. For an excellent explication of how this can be done, cf. Mazower (2006) and his retelling of the story of Thessaloniki.
13. Also consider the internet project, linking stories across the world (Heinich, Molenda, Russell, & Smaldino, 1999); http://www.library.yale.edu/testimonies/homepage.html
14. http://library.mcneese.edu/depts/archive/mediterr108.htm
15. http://www.med-voices.org/pages/index.aspx
16. In March 2005, the workshop 'Constructions of Mediterranean Nostalgia' was held at the University of Athens, reaffirming the constructedness of Mediterranean memories. And in May of the same year, the conference 'Inscriptions' was held at Eastern Mediterranean University. It included several panels on revisionist histories, memory and forgetting. In May 2007, the conference 'Armenian Memory' was held in Lyon, dealing largely with Armenian Diasporas and the function of memory within them. And, lastly, in November 2008 PRIO Cyprus hosted a conference entitled 'One Island, Many Histories: Rethinking the Politics of the Past in Cyprus'. While its focus was of course Cyprus, many approaches to the (re-)framing of memories in the light of contested memory territories are also applicable to the wider Eastern Mediterranean.
17. As an example, consider Landolf Scherzer's 2005 *Der Grenzgänger* (The Border Rambler). In his reportage, the author wanders the length of the stretch of land that until 1989 used to be the German–German border. Through his low-key and conversational narrative, he is able to understand and portray people living along this once impenetrable border. And he readily acknowledges that the willingness of his respondents was mostly due to the fact that they felt he was one of them.

References

Abrams, L. (2010). *Oral history theory.* London: Routledge.

Anderson, B. (2006). *Imagined communities.* London: Verso.

Baldwin, M., & Lopez, D.F. (1990). Priming relationship schemas: My advisor and the Pope are watching me from the back of my mind. *Journal of Experimental Social Psychology, 26,* 434–451.

Bamford, A. (2011). *The Visual Literacy White Paper.* Retrieved October 14, 2012, from http://www.adobe.com/uk/education/pdf/adobe_visual_literacy_paper.pdf

Briel, H. (2008). The will to media. In H. Briel (Ed.), *Glocalisation. Electronic media in South-Eastern Europe* (pp. 13–28). Skopje: Blesok.

Briel, H. (2012). Blogging and online subjectivities. In R. Parkin-Gounelas (Ed.), *The psychology and politics of the collective* (pp. 168–182). London: Routledge.

Brown, K.S. (2003). *The past in question: Modern Macedonia and the uncertainties of nation.* Princeton, NJ: Princeton University Press.

Butler, B. (2009). *Return to Alexandria. An ethnography of cultural heritage revivalism and museum memory.* Oxford: Berg.

Canefe, N. (2006). *Milliyetcilik, Kimlik ve Aidiyet* [Nationalism, identity and belonging]. Istanbul: Bilgi University Publishing House.

Canefe, N. (Ed.) (2007). *The Jewish diaspora as a paradigm: Politics, religion and belonging.* Lewiston, NY: Mellen.

Dawson, G., Rogers, K.L., & Leydesdorff, S. (Eds.). (1999). *Trauma and life stories.* London: Routledge.

Denis, P. (2007). The ethics of oral history in South Africa. *Journal of the Eastern and Southern Africa Regional Branch of the International Council on Archives, 26.* Retrieved October 14, 2012, from http://www.ajol.info/index.php/esarjo/article/view/31017

Field, S. (2012). *Oral history, community, and displacement. Imagining memories in post-apartheid South Africa.* London: Palgrave.

Frank, G. (1995). Anthropology and individual lives: The story of life history and the history of the life story. *American Anthropologist, 97*(1), 145–149.

Frisch, M. (1989). *A shared authority: Essays on the craft and meaning of oral and public history.* New York: SUNY Press.

Giorgis, C., Johnson, N.J., Bonono, A., Colberg, C., Conner, A., & Kauffman, G. (1999). Visual literacy. *Reading Teacher, 53*(2), 146–153.

Goody, J. (2007). *The theft of history.* Cambridge: Cambridge University Press.

Hamilton, P., & Shopes, L. (Eds.). (2008). *Oral history and public memory.* Philadelphia: Temple University Press.

Haugbolle, S. (2005). Public and private memory of the Lebanese Civil War. *Comparative Studies of South Asia, Africa and the Middle East, 25*(1), 191–203.

Heinich, R., Molenda, M., Russell, J.D., & Smaldino, S. (1999). *World Internet Project.* Retrieved October 14, 2012, from http://www.worldinternetproject.org

Hodgkin, K., & Radstone, S. (Eds.). (2003). *Contested pasts: The politics of memory.* London: Routledge.

Kaufman, S.J. (2004). *Selective memory and the politics of myth-making in the Israeli–Palestinian conflict.* Paper presented at the annual meeting of the International Studies Association, Le Centre Sheraton Hotel, Montreal, Quebec, Canada. Retrieved October 14, 2012, from http://www.allacademic.com/meta/p74598_index.html

Kovacs, E. (2006, May 22). The mémoire croisée of the Shoah. *Eurozine.* Retrieved October 14, 2012, from http://www.eurozine.com/articles/2006-05-22-kovacs-en.html

Leventis, Y. (2002). *Cyprus: The struggle for self-determination in the1940s. Prelude to deeper crisis.* Bern: Lang.

Leventis, Y., Murata, N., & Hazama, Y. (2008). *Crossing over Cyprus: Studies on the divided island in the Eastern Mediterranean.* Tokyo: Tokyo University of Foreign Studies.

Linde, C. (1983). *Life stories: The creation of coherence.* Oxford: Oxford University Press.

Makdidi, U.S. (2000). *The culture of sectarianism: Community, history, and violence in nineteenth-century Ottoman Lebanon.* Berkeley: University of California Press.

Makdidi, U.S. (Ed.). (2006). *Memory and violence in the Middle East and North Africa.* Bloomington: Indiana University Press.

Mazower, M. (2006). *Salonica, city of ghosts: Christians, Muslims and Jews 1430–1950*. New York: Vintage.

Merikle, P.M., & Daneman, M. (1998). Psychological investigations of unconscious perception. *Journal of Consciousness Studies, 5*(1), 5–18.

Meskell, L. (Ed.). (1998). *Archaeology under fire: Nationalism, politics and heritage in the Eastern Mediterranean and Middle East*. London: Routledge.

Meyerhoff, B. (Ed.). (1992). *Remembered lives: The work of ritual, storytelling and growing older*. Ann Arbor: University of Michigan Press.

Nadjarian, N. (2006). *Ledra Street*. Nicosia: Armida.

Nair-Venugopal, S. (2009). Interculturalities: Reframing identities in intercultural communication. *Language and Intercultural Communication, 9*(2), 76–90.

Nuttall, S., & Coetzee, C. (Eds.). (1998). *Negotiating the past: The making of memory in South Africa*. Cape Town: Oxford University Press.

Öztürkmen, A. (2006). Remembering conflicts in a Black Sea town: A multi-sited ethnography of memory. *New Perspectives on Turkey, 34*, 93–115.

Papadakis, Y. (2005). *Echoes from the dead zone: Across the Cyprus divide*. London: Tauris.

Papadakis, Y. (2006). Aphrodite delights. *Postcolonial Studies, 9*(3), 237–250.

Passerine, L. (1979). Work, ideology and consensus under Italian fascism. *History Workshop Journal, 8*, 82–108.

Portelli, A. (1997). *The Battle of Valle Giulia: Oral history and the art of dialogue*. Madison: University of Wisconsin Press.

Sa'di, A.H., & Abu-Lughod, L. (Eds.). (2007). *Nakba: Palestine, 1948, and the claims of memory*. New York: Columbia University Press.

Saeed, S. (2009). Negotiating power: Community media, democracy, and the public sphere. *Development in Practice, 19*(4), 466–478.

Schacter, D. (1996). *Searching for memory*. New York: Basic Books.

Scherzer, L. (2005). *Der Grenzgänger*. Berlin: Aufbau.

Scott, J. (2002). World heritage as a model for citizenship: The case of Cyprus. *International Journal of Heritage Studies, 2*(1), 99–115.

Sinatra, R. (1986). *Visual literacy connections to thinking, reading and writing*. Springfield, IL: Charles C. Thomas.

Stokes, S. (2001). Visual literacy in teaching and learning: A literature perspective. *Electronic Journal for the Integration of Technology in Education, 1*(1). Retrieved October 14, 2012, from http://ejite.isu.edu/Volume1No1/Stokes.html

Stoler, A.L. (with Strassler, K.). (2006). Memory-work in Java: A cautionary tale. In R. Perks & A. Thomson (Eds.), *The oral history reader* (2nd ed., pp. 283–310). London: Routledge.

The Armenian Diaspora. Retrieved October 14, 2012, from http://www.armeniadiaspora.com

The Memory Bank. Retrieved October 14, 2012, from http://www.thememorybank.co.uk

Troebst, S. (2001). *Historical politics and historical 'masterpieces' in Macedonia before and after 1991*. Retrieved October 14, 2012, from http://www.newbalkanpolitics.org.mk/OldSite/Issue_6/troebst.historical.eng.asp

UK Oral History Society. Retrieved October 14, 2012, from www.oralhistory.org.uk

US Oral History Association. Retrieved October 14, 2012, from www.oralhistory.org

Volk, L. (2008). When memory repeats itself: The politics of heritage in post civil war Lebanon. *International Journal of Middle East Studies, 40*, 291–314.

Wileman, R.E. (1993). *Visual communicating*. Englewood Cliffs, NJ: Educational Technology Publications.

Beyond the reach of ethics and equity? Depersonalisation and dehumanisation in foreign domestic helper narratives

Hans J. Ladegaard

Department of English, Hong Kong Baptist University, Ho Sin Hang Campus, Waterloo Road, Kowloon Tong, Hong Kong

This paper analyses narratives told by foreign domestic helpers (FDHs) in a Hong Kong church shelter. The narratives provide evidence that FDHs appear to be untouched by the ethics and equity of Hong Kong society. They are denied the rights that apply to other groups: the right to eat, rest and talk; they are humiliated and denigrated, and the analyses show that this treatment may affect their self-perception. The paper considers local stereotypes and ideological representations as a possible cause for legitimising the exploitation of FDHs, and it recommends that researchers become engaged in social activism in the attempt to help FDHs rewrite their narratives of repression.

本文作者於教會收容所訪問了大量外籍家庭傭工, 他們的敘述
證實, 香港社會的道德標準及公正的氛圍並未觸及外籍傭工的生活狀況。
他們不僅無法像其他族群一樣, 享受飲食, 休息及談話這樣的基本人權
, 還要忍受著雇主的羞辱與誣衊。研究表明這樣的不公平待遇或影響外
籍傭工的自我認同。本文旨在論證本地偏見及意識形態表現在某種程度
上使剝削合理化, 並鼓勵更多研究者參與社會運動, 改善外傭
的生活狀況, 改寫他們的故事。

Introduction

On 4 May 2010, a 28-year-old Indonesian domestic helper comes to Bethune House, a church shelter for foreign domestic helpers (FDHs) in Hong Kong. She is visibly distraught, telling the staff that she has run away from her employer with no luggage and no money. Maryane[1] worked for four months for an abusive employer who beat her every day; she worked 18 hours a day on very little food, and had to sleep inside the toilet. As the story unfolds, with detailed accounts of how she is beaten and dragged by the hair across the kitchen floor, she sobs and is barely capable of speaking. This is a story of unspeakable suffering and humiliation, a trauma narrative whose tellability is compromised by the unacceptability of the events (Shuman, 2005, pp. 19–20). Unlike many FDH narratives, Maryane's story is documented which makes it even more compelling, and the cruelty of the employer more unfathomable. She recorded the beatings, and her employer yelling at her, on her mobile phone, and after the abuse, she used her mobile phone to take pictures of her swollen face and bruises. The volunteer is in shock as he looks through dozens of pictures of swollen lips and eyes, bleedings from nose and ears, and bruises all over her face. For four months, she did not leave the house, and for four months, she was beaten every day. The excerpt below is a transcript of one of the beatings which Maryane recorded on her mobile phone. She has laid the table for breakfast, but has forgotten to put the butter (and apparently other things) on the table (voice of female employer; original in Cantonese; transcription conventions in the Appendix).

Excerpt 1
what is missing? what is missing? (2.0) huh? (2.0) anything? what is missing? anything? [slap] anything? huh? [slap] why can't you [slap] take a look? [slap] can't you take a look first? [slap] to see what is missing before you do the laundry? [...] maybe the butter is missing, then bring it out, I didn't ask you to toast the bread, what's wrong with you? should I get angry again tomorrow? (2.0) I have reminded you **many times**, you have a poor memory, then you should check, if anything is missing (1.0) huh? (3.0) you better **die** [slap] why aren't you **dead**? you better jump off the building and kill yourself, you better die (3.0) you make me so angry every day, you better die

Like the Abu Ghraib incidents discussed in Caton (2010, p. 166), Maryane's story represents 'a limit case in our thinking on ethics'. It somehow exceeds 'what we might call the "unethical" and might be better captured under the category of evil'. Although modern philosophy and anthropology have virtually abandoned evil as an analytical concept (and consigned it to theology), it seems appropriate to reintroduce it to characterise intentionally demeaning behaviour which appears to serve no other purpose but to humiliate and dehumanise another human being. This paper explores intercultural discourses that move beyond the reach of ethics and equity as it were. 'Intercultural discourses' here refer to FDHs' accounts of how their employers construct them as 'different', and as abject and out of place – that is, as evidence of the demonisation of the cultural Other. Thus, interculturality is conceptualised primarily as 'material inequalities, power relations, and ideological difference, rather than simply skin color, geographical location, [and] passport ...' (Thurlow, 2010, p. 241). The paper analyses narratives of and about ethnic minority group members who appear to be untouched by the ethics and equity that normally apply to Hong Kong society. Therefore, these concepts cease to be meaningful, and this emphasises first, the need for the researcher to redefine his own role and, ultimately, become a social activist as well as a researcher, and second, the need to reconceptualise the participants who become something more than research subjects. Scholars have argued that a sharp distinction between research commitment and social commitment cannot be upheld in projects that involve marginalised and underprivileged groups (Shuman, 2005; Solis, 2004). Therefore, this paper advocates that research on domestic helper narratives should not just do research *on* FDHs, but also *for* and *with* them (Cameron, Fraser, Harvey, Rampton, & Richardson, 1992).

In the narratives, Filipina and Indonesian domestic workers give their accounts of how they have been dehumanised by their employers' racist demeaning discourses. Storytelling is important because it accomplishes a variety of interactional goals, but narratives also serve a deeper psychological function. People use them to make sense of their world: 'through life stories individuals and groups make sense of themselves; they tell what they are or what they wish to be, as they tell so they become, they *are* their stories' (Cortazzi, 2001, p. 388). Furthermore, FDH narratives are stories that

45

simply need to be told and brought to the public's attention. Many domestic workers in Hong Kong (and elsewhere) have been silenced by years of repression and abuse. Narratives of suffering must (like any other type of research) explicitly state the purpose of such research, but in addition, 'they insist, sometimes even more explicitly than the scientific rationale, on knowledge as redemption and on the possibility that telling untold stories might make a better world' (Shuman, 2005, p. 162).

The paper gives first, a brief summary of the theoretical and methodological frameworks which have informed the research. Second, it gives a brief account of the church shelter as a research site, followed by a discourse analysis of excerpts from selected domestic helper narratives. Finally, it discusses FDH narratives as evidence of the depersonalisation[2] and dehumanisation of certain groups in society, and it considers the 'local codes of argument' (Tileaga, 2005), that is, the predominant stereotypes and ideological representations in the macro context which may legitimise the exploitation of FDHs.

Theoretical and methodological frameworks

The project draws on a variety of theoretical frameworks and analytical concepts from sociolinguistics, pragmatics and discourse analysis. The data was collected using an ethnography-of-communication approach (Saville-Troike, 2003) which emphasises the need to observe the research site and collect contextual information to assist the fieldworker in the interpretation of spoken data. Another framework which has been important for understanding the nature of discourse in the church shelter is social constructionism (Burr, 1995). This approach recognises the situated nature and dynamic aspect of talk, and it argues that in social interaction, people present and negotiate their social identities, as well as their social group memberships and group boundaries. Thus, talk is seen as a site for identity construction, and people are seen as constantly being engaged in a dynamic process of negotiating aspects of their interpersonal and intergroup identity (Holmes, 2006). A social constructionist approach to narrative research would see narratives as a 'situated, co-constructed interaction between interviewer and participant, and with identities as their product, or process' (Benwell & Stokoe, 2006, p. 143). It examines people's lives holistically by analysing their stories, and the analyst would ask questions such as: Why was this narrative told and why did it develop the way it did? How does the narrator make identity claims and what other identities are being suggested? How did the audience (other FDHs and volunteers) respond and how did that influence the development of the story? (cf. Riessman, 2003).

The narratives have been analysed using a narrative-analysis approach combining Toolan's attention to linguistic detail (2001) with the therapeutic component of narrative research which other studies have emphasised (e.g. Brown & Augusta-Scott, 2007; Payne, 2006). Narrative therapy emphasises that we live storied lives and therefore, people are encouraged to tell their stories so that they can make sense of their past experiences because 'our stories do not simply represent us or mirror lived events – they constitute us, shaping our lives and our relationships' (Brown & Augusta-Scott, 2007, p. ix). Many scholars refer to five key functions of storytelling (see Medved & Brockmeier, 2008). First, it creates coherence by synthesising personal experiences that may appear disconnected. Second, storytelling serves a distancing function, that is, the narrator distances herself from the immediacy of her (traumatic) experiences by converting them to stories. Third, narratives serve a communicative function: they connect the narrator to her audience so that the narrator's universe becomes shared. Fourth, stories help narrators evaluate past events; they provide perspective and the opportunity to re-evaluate and come up with alternative interpretations. Finally, narratives serve an explorative function: they encourage the narrator to explore two sides of human experience – the real and the possible. This is particularly important in FDH narratives because the women at the shelter are encouraged to question the dominant discourses they have been subjected to in their employers' houses and seek to 're-author their lives from victimhood to survival and beyond' (Duvall & Béres, 2007, p. 233).

The church shelter as a research site

The church shelter offers temporary accommodation to FDHs whose contract has been terminated, or who have run away from abusive employers. Despite legislation designed to protect FDHs, many are exploited and abused (Chiu, 2005; Constable, 2007; Ladegaard, 2012, in press), and because many are not aware of their rights, the employers may get away with months of abuse before it is discovered. When FDHs arrive at the church shelter, they are invited to share their story with other helpers and a volunteer in a sharing session. The purpose of these sessions is first, to clarify the details of a particular case and provide the necessary documentation in case a FDH needs to file a complaint to the Labour Department or the police, and second, to serve a therapeutic function by providing the women with an opportunity to talk about their traumas in a non-threatening environment.

I joined the shelter as a volunteer in 2008, but I soon realised that these narratives needed to be documented and shared with a wider audience. Therefore, the project was converted into a research-based study of migrant worker narratives, while I continued to work as a volunteer for the shelter. I am aware of the problems involved in fulfilling two roles simultaneously. First, the role of the researcher who is trying to observe and analyse language without 'contaminating' the social environment I am studying, and second, the role of the volunteer whose job it is to document the stories and encourage the women to talk about their traumas. I am under no illusion that I can be a 'neutral' observer; I am on the side of the domestic workers and I make no secret of that. I am also clear about the ultimate goal of this research: it is action research which attempts to advance a social justice research agenda in intercultural communication. Jackson and Moshin (2010, p. 361) argue that being a critical intercultural scholar is inherently political, 'because it is ideology and hegemony that create the[se] differences which we are trying to expose, the[se] injustices that we are trying to change'. Thus, I see myself as a social activist *and* a researcher and would argue that these roles may be complimentary rather than contradictory. In the sharing sessions, I take on the role of the interviewer who asks questions, mainly to document the details of a particular case, but I also try to act as a facilitator who offers advice and encourages the participants to take action against their abusive employers.

Each week, I would meet with newcomers who had signed up for a sharing session (usually a group of four to six women). I would explain the research and the social activism component of the study and ask for participants' consent to use the narratives for research purposes. They were granted full anonymity and promised that any information in the narratives which might compromise their (or their employers') identity would be deleted. Most FDHs would stay at the shelter for about two weeks and would therefore participate in only one sharing session. Unless a domestic worker has a pending court case, or a case with the Labour Tribunal, she must leave Hong Kong no later than two weeks after her contract was terminated. Several long-term residents at the shelter, who were waiting for their case to be heard, became more involved in the sharing sessions, either as interpreters or simply as more experienced FDHs who would give an update on their case and thus, encourage others to file a complaint against abusive employers.

Despite the fleeting nature of the relationship between researcher and FDH, the sharing sessions were generally informal and relaxed and yet, characterised by great intimacy. Any fears I might have had before I joined the shelter that the women would be reluctant to share their stories with a white male researcher were brought to shame. For most newcomers, the sharing session was the first opportunity given to them to share their story (sometimes after months with an abusive employer) and most of them seized the opportunity without hesitation. In some sharing sessions, only I participated with the newcomers; in others, Filipina or Indonesian volunteers, or local social workers doing their practicum at the shelter, would also participate.

The two dominant groups of FDHs in the shelter, Filipinas and Indonesians, are quite different in terms of their social characteristics. The average Filipina domestic helper tends to be mature, well educated, married with children and has often lived abroad for many years. This means she is usually perfectly fluent in English, and it is no surprise therefore, that the Filipinas opted for English in the sharing sessions. The average Indonesian helper, on the other hand, tends to be younger, single and with little or no formal education. This means that many Indonesians do not speak much English, and sharing sessions with them therefore had to be conducted with the help of interpreters (usually a volunteer or another FDH) using a mix of English, Bahasa and Javanese. The recordings with the Indonesians were transcribed and translated by two Indonesian students who were fluent in all three languages. As of June 2012, 53 sharing sessions have been recorded involving a total of 220 FDHs; about 30 of them have been transcribed and, for the Indonesian data, translated. Each session usually lasts between 60 and 90 minutes.

Analysis of data

In the examples selected for analysis in this paper, the employers' dehumanisation of FDHs is in focus. Excerpt 2 is from a sharing session with six Indonesian domestic workers and an interpreter. A male interviewer[3]/volunteer is present in all the excerpts quoted in this paper. The women are explaining what went wrong with their previous employers.

Excerpt 2
Sendy, 24 years old, 5 months in HK; Lintang, 37 years old, 9 months in HK, 3 years in Taiwan before; Utari, 33 years old, 9 months in HK, 2 years in Malaysia before; Sarawasti, 25 years old, 5 months in HK. Three more Indonesian FDHs and an interpreter (Sinta), were in this sharing session. Original in Bahasa & English.

1.	Sen:	I came to Hong Kong on 6 December (0.9) 2008, my employer was kind for the
2.		first and second month but after that (1.6) she became so bad, she always cut my
3.		salary and she hit me three times (0.5) if the door is broken I have to fix it, if the
4.		pipe is broken I also have to fix it (0.8) when it's my holiday [Sunday] I leave at
5.		12 and have to be back by eight but I usually come back before eight (0.8) they
6.		don't give me a key so sometimes I fall asleep for three or four hours in front of
7.		the house before they open the door for me (2.0) and they don't allow me to use
8.		hot water [for showers] (Bahasa) [...]

9.	Int:	why do you think (1.0) people (0.5) treat you like that? Why are you (0.8) being
10.		treated like that by your employer? Why have (1.3) why? (0.9) (English)
11.	Sin:	what's on your mind, why did the employer do this to you? (1.6) (Bahasa)
12.	Lin:	maybe because I don't have any work experience in Hong Kong before (0.5) so
13.		maybe my employer (0.9) thinks I'm stupid (0.5) don't understand anything (1.7)
14.		maybe that's why they don't give me any holiday (0.9) I might get influenced by
15.		my friends, so that's why I didn't get any holiday, even public holidays (1.7)
16.		(Bahasa)
17.	Uta:	my employer said (0.5) domestic helpers are stupid, dirty (0.5) rotten (0.5) so we
18.		are not worthy to (0.6) be respected (3.0) (Bahasa)
19	Sar:	because this is my first time so I couldn't (0.5) speak Cantonese yet (0.5) so my
20.		employer said (0.7) 'you've been here for two months, why can't you speak
21.		Cantonese?' (0.7) they said I'm stupid (0.8) that's what they said (Bahasa) […]
22.	Lin:	[sighs] my employer loves to say I can't do anything, my work is always wrong
23.		(0.5) my employer said (0.5) I'm useless, cannot speak the language (0.5) even
24.		though I (0.5) my employer said I cannot cook and they complained to the agent
25.		(0.5) although I have paid attention to the cooking, I even wrote everything down
26.		so I'm sure I can do it, but my employer keeps saying I'm useless […] (Bahasa)

Several themes are brought up in these women's stories. First, in Sendy's narrative, the employer's demeaning behaviour through physical assaults and salary reduction. In Chiu's extensive quantitative research among a representative sample of 2500 FDHs in Hong Kong (2005), almost 20% of the Filipinas and almost 40% of the Indonesians, reported to have been physically assaulted by their employer at least once. This demeaning behaviour is of course inexcusable and unacceptable, but, according to Constable (2007), should not primarily be seen as examples of racism, but rather, as examples of how FDHs are perceived in Hong Kong: as commodities who can be 'inspected, bought, traded, generally objectified, and treated as economic investments' (p. 51). Like the Chinese *amahs*, foreign domestic workers are expected to be subservient and obey their masters without question, and because they are perceived as their employers' property, they can also be punished if they disobey.

Underpayment is another common problem for FDHs, and another means for employers to denigrate their helpers. Reducing domestic workers' legal minimum wage is a way to effectively belittle them and deprive them of the recognition their work deserves. Chui (2005) found that 50% of the Indonesian workers in his sample were underpaid; Filipinas are less likely to be underpaid, presumably because they tend to be more informed about their rights. Taylor (1994, p. 25) argues that non-recognition 'can be a form of oppression, imprisoning someone in a false, distorted, and reduced mode of being'. When asked why they are being mistreated by their employers, Lintang says 'because I don't have any work experience' (l. 12), and in another sharing session, Doreen, a 24-year-old helper from the Philippines, responds to the same question by saying: 'because this is my first time in Hong Kong, so maybe I cannot adjust, so maybe next time (2.0) uh: maybe there's more improvement'. This is supported by Indah, a 29-year-old Indonesian domestic worker, who adds: 'I want to improve in the future […] so perhaps I will be treated better' (original in Bahasa). These women's responses demonstrate how many FDHs position themselves: as responsible for the demeaning discourses they have experienced in their employers' houses. These women blame themselves and therefore conclude that they are 'not worthy to be respected' (l. 18). Thus, through society's lack of recognition of their work, and through their employers' demeaning discourses, these women have internalised a picture of their own inferiority.

Another means of dehumanising FDHs is depriving them of their statutory holidays. Domestic workers are entitled to one day off per week, as well as all public holidays, but stories like Lintang's (ll. 14–15) are common. She worked 16–18 hours per day for nine months without one single day off, and she suspects the reason is that her employer did not want her to socialise with other FDHs and learn about her rights. In Chiu's study (2005), 63% of Indonesian domestic workers reported that they did not get their mandatory holidays, 'a situation of virtual slavery' (p. 27), and a problem for a significant majority of Indonesians.

Another theme in the narratives in Excerpt 1 is the verbal denigration which is a salient feature in many FDH narratives. The maids are being referred to as 'stupid, dirty, rotten' (l. 17) and 'useless' (l. 23) because they cannot speak Cantonese, or because they do not excel in Cantonese cooking (ll. 19–21 & 23–26). Based on these derogatory characteristics, the women perceive themselves as 'not worthy to be respected' (l. 18). De Fina (2006, pp. 353–354) argues that 'the identities that people display, perform, contest, or discuss in interaction are based on ideologies and beliefs about the characteristics of social groups and categories and about the implications of belonging to them'. This means that these women's narrative self-construction is closely interrelated with predominant stereotypes and ideological representations of FDHs in Hong Kong. If employers construct narratives about domestic workers as 'useless', 'dirty' and 'stupid', these narratives are likely to affect the women's own stories so that they construct themselves as inferior members of the community (see Ladegaard, 2012; Taylor, 1994).

In the next excerpt, a group of Filipina domestic workers are discussing their daily routines when they worked for their previous employer. They have all had their contract terminated.

Excerpt 3
Tala, 48 years old, 5 months in HK, 8 years in Taiwan & 1 year in Egypt before HK;
Eloise, 43 years old, 7 months in HK, 2 years in Singapore & 8 years in Taiwan before HK;
Jovely, 24 years old, 5 months in HK. One more Filipina helper was in this sharing session.
Original in English.

1.	Tala:	I start work at 6 in the morning, and then until 12 or sometimes 1, she doesn't
2.		want me to take a rest
3.	Inv:	okay
4.	Tala:	from sunrise to sunset
5.	Inv:	work all the time?
6.	Elo:	yeah, also my employer is like that
7.	Jov:	also my employer, I wake up at 5 and then I take a bath and prepare myself xx I
8.		start preparing breakfast because the children need to go to school at 6 (1.0) then I
9.		do laundry, cleaning cooking xx I sleep around 11 something, every day, the
10.		whole day, no sleep
11.	Inv:	no sleep, no break?
12.	Jov:	no break, only lunch, but standing also
13.	Inv:	so you have to stand while you eat?
14.	Elo:	me also, my employer [laughs]
15.	Jov:	5 minutes
16.	Elo:	me too, my employer says, '15 minutes only (0.5) if you **must** eat' (1.0) 15
17.		minutes **only** and then after that, work again
18.	Inv:	okay
19.	Elo:	work work work, and sometimes err my employer's asking me to comb her hair
20.		[…] I comb her hair, two hours, I stand for two hours just combing her hair, until
21.		it becomes dry [general laughter] and she makes telephone calls and she says 'I'm
22.		too tired, you can brush my hair', like that, 'okay' I say, then I brush

Excerpt 3 provides another example of the employers' depersonalisation and dehumanisation of FDHs. They are treated, not like human beings, but as any other inanimate household appliance. All FDHs at the shelter are asked about their working hours, and the average for the vast majority is at least 16 hours a day. An average day for a domestic helper is 'work, work, work' (l. 19) and no rest. Even at mealtimes, they are usually offered very little food (if anything at all), and they have to stand while they eat. The comment from Eloise's employer, '15 minutes only, if you **must** eat' (l. 16), is telling. FDHs are deprived of their basic needs, and the underlying assumption is that they ought to be able to function without food, like a robot. The BOGOF (Buy-One-Get-One-Free) rule testifies to the same reality. Most agencies in Hong Kong have an unwritten rule that allows the employer to try out a new domestic helper for three months, and if s/he is not satisfied, return her to the agency and get a new maid for free. Domestic helpers are perceived as commodities; like faulty goods, they can be returned before the warranty expires if the buyer is not satisfied. The BOGOF scam may work well for the employer and the agency, but is detrimental to FDHs who have to find another employer within two weeks, and, in some cases, start over with extortionate agency fees[4] or they will be deported.

Constable (1997, p. 553) argues that:

> employers' discipline and control of domestic workers can also be seen as an attempt to reduce them to docile social bodies, to deprive them of full personhood, and to craft for them a less morally ambivalent – but sufficiently subordinate – position within the household.

She further argues that the loss of status and control for many women in Chinese families is the key to understanding why they humiliate their helpers. Because of the helpers, they have lost the status they once enjoyed as head of the household, and with husbands who work long hours and children preoccupied with school work, these women, who see their position threatened by the presence of a domestic helper, may get some degree of satisfaction and self-aggrandisement through the humiliation and denigration of their helper (see Ladegaard, 2012; Zimbardo, 2007). Thus, controlling their helpers 'offers them one way of continuing to exert authority' (Constable, 1997, p. 553). The maids' services are not just confined to domestic work: after 16 hours or more in the kitchen, it is common to ask them to do a massage, manicure or, as in Eloise's case, comb her employer's hair. In other more extreme cases, FDHs are expected to perform sexual services in the bedroom after 16 hours of housework in the kitchen (see Ladegaard, in press). The dehumanisation of FDHs is also evident in the next excerpt.

Excerpt 4
Madalyn, Filipina, 25 years old, 2 months in HK; Vanessa, Filipina, 41 years old, 18 months in HK, 14 years in Singapore before HK. Four more Filipinas were in this sharing session.
1. Mad: I have to time my use of the toilet, she wants me to use the toilet [from] 7 o'clock
2. in the morning to 7:30, sometimes you can't arrange your time, you cannot use
3. the toilet [from] 7 to 7:30, if it's er: 8 o'clock, and you're gonna use the toilet,
4. she's so very angry with me
5. Int: okay
6. Mad: she's very angry, sometimes when she asks me to go out and buy bread for the: for
7. the kids (1.0) because the building under us is the mall, shopping mall, I use the
8. toilet in the shopping mall, when I'm back, 'why are you so long?' (2.0) I feel

9.   like, I don't know [laughs] I feel like a robot sir
10. Van: we are not robots [general laughter]
11. Mad: I feel like a robot, even when you're eating, you have no time (1.5) you just wait,
12.   just wait like a cat or a dog, you just wait and see what they put on your plate
13. Inv: yeah
14. Mad: we're sleeping with our stomachs [grrrrrr] [makes a noise]
15. Van: rumbling [general laughter]

The metaphors picked by these women to illustrate how they feel they are being positioned occur frequently in domestic helper narratives. They are being positioned by their employers as robots (l. 9) whose functions can be timed so that they deliver a particular output between 7 and 7:30, or as dogs or cats waiting by their troughs to be fed (l. 12). The laughter in l. 9 may serve as a face-saving device, or as a means of expressing the tragi-comic aspect in their situation (Ladegaard, in press), whereas the laughter in ll. 10 & 15 is, more likely, a laughter of amusement which might also function as an ingroup solidarity marker (Holmes & Marra, 2002). There are also discourses of resistance in this excerpt, voiced particularly by Vanessa who refuses to accept the forced identity of a docile domestic worker. When FDHs voice opposition to forced identities and begin to redefine their own situation, they may also be empowered to re-author their narratives and become agents in their own life-stories (De Fina & Baynham, 2005). Vanessa's narrative illustrates this development. She worked for the same employer for 18 months; she worked 16–18 hours every day with no breaks. She had to sneak to the toilet just to sit down for five minutes and eat a biscuit, and when her employer began to demean her with comments like 'How could you stay 14 years in Singapore with no brain?', she answered back: 'I never encountered that with my employers in Singapore, none of my employers tell me that so I answer back.' Subsequently, Vanessa's contract is terminated, but she has made a statement: 'We are helpers, we are not slaves', and thus, she becomes an inspiration to other FDHs in this sharing session that they do not have to accept that their life-stories are written exclusively by the employer.

Madalyn's use of the polite address form 'sir' (l. 9) also deserves a comment. It is common for FDHs to use 'Sir'/'Madam' when they address their employers, and it also happens in the sharing sessions when they address the volunteers. It is possible they use it to signal deference and perceived inferiority, but it is perhaps more likely an automated response, a polite respectful term of address, which the women use without attaching much meaning to it. This interpretation is supported by the fact that I, when I first joined the shelter, frequently requested not to be called 'Sir' but by my first name, and although the women always complied, they soon forgot. This suggests that polite forms of address are internalised in their vocabulary and used without much awareness.

The last excerpt demonstrates another aspect of life for FDHs: a life of loneliness and isolation. Excerpt 5 is from a sharing session with five FDHs from the Philippines. They are discussing why their contract was terminated.

Excerpt 5
Beryl, 37 years old, 3 months in HK, 2 years in Singapore before HK; Flordeliza, 46 years old, 3 years in HK, 3 years in Taiwan before HK; Alma, 33 years old, 1 week in HK, 3 years in Jordan before HK. Two more Filipinas were in this sharing session.
1. Ber: my employer is very strict, just because she saw me talk to another Filipina
2.   but the truth is I didn't talk her, she just **say** I talked to her, but no, it's not true [...]

3.	Inv:	and you're not supposed to talk?
4.	Ber:	not to another maid because I took her [someone working in the same house]
5.		to the supermarket because I had something to carry and then some Filipina
6.		came and suddenly she asked me 'where is my employer, is she inside the
7.		supermarket or not?', but I didn't answer and suddenly my employer got out
8.		and she saw the Filipina talk to me, so she think that I talked to her
9.	Inv:	and you're not allowed to talk to another//
10:	Ber:	//that's right
11.	Al:	yeah
12.	Ber:	that's just the reason [for terminating her employment]
13.	Inv:	is that (1.0) have you experienced the same thing? (1.0) that you're not
14.		allowed to talk to other (1.0)
15.	Al:	most, most are like this
16.	Flor:	yeah yeah, most employers don't want their helper to talk//
17.	Al:	//also my employer [...]
18.		because she is a teacher, tutor, so some other Filipinas go with the children to
19.		have tutoring there with my employer and then when they come, my employer
20.		say to me 'don't talk to her', like this

Sampson (1993) argues that one of the greatest promises of discourse is that it offers us the opportunity 'to converse with others and to learn about our own otherness in and through those conversations' (p. 186). Only in discourse do we become truly human; only in dialogue do we get to know the Other, but perhaps more importantly, only in dialogue do we get to know ourselves through our interlocutors' affirmation of our value. In discourse, our uniqueness is communicated to us, and if individuals are deprived of discourse, they not only become lonely and isolated, but they also lose their self-worth. Tajfel (1981) found that membership of ingroups, and the positive values attached to these memberships, are essential, not only to the individual's well-being, but to his/her survival. So depriving individuals of discourse is also to deprive them of their sense of belonging, and to deprive them of their self-worth and confidence – in short, depriving them of their humanity.

Another reason for denying FDHs the right to talk to each other is that they might learn about their rights (see Lintang's comment, Excerpt 2, ll. 14–15). Lonely isolated employees are easier to control, and the fact that Indonesian helpers, who tend not to be organised, are generally more severely exploited than Filipinas, suggests that isolation is an effective way to keep FDHs ignorant of their rights. Constable (2007, p. 12) makes an important point about domestic workers and resistance. She argues that power does not exist in a monolithic, autonomous and 'natural state' until it becomes fractured by acts of resistance. In other words, 'power and resistance coexist and constantly reassert themselves against each other' (p. 13). This means that in order to avoid a challenge from FDHs to their claim to undisputed absolute power, employers need to prevent domestic workers from communicating and supporting each other.

Discussion

FDH narratives provide ample evidence of the repression of voice (Bloomfield, 2000), and about the victimisation of certain minority groups in Hong Kong society. In order to understand this phenomenon, we need to look not just at discourse but also at the wider socio-cultural context. As argued by Verkuyten (2001, p. 275), '[the] wider ideological context is both inside and outside talk', so in order to understand the dehumanisation of FDHs, we need to see narratives as evidence of 'the "lived ideology", the local codes of argument, the cultural and ideological resources used to account for controversial issues such as prejudice, discrimination and inequality' (Tileaga, 2005, p. 606). Hong Kong prides itself on being *Asia's World City*, a city of opportunities, peaceful coexistence between different ethnic groups, and widespread tolerance of different religions, languages and cultures. So how is it possible that this cosmopolitan city, which could, in some respects, be seen as model for cross-cultural understanding and tolerance, apparently also fosters extreme prejudice against certain groups?

Tileaga (2007) argues that we need to examine ideologies of moral exclusion in order to understand how certain groups become conceptualised as legitimate outcasts. He discusses the concept of ontologisation which 'refers to the representation of certain minorities outside the social realm, outside the realm of "humanity"' – in other words, 'a psychological mechanism to achieve social exclusion' (p. 719). Dehumanising certain groups involves psychologically removing them from the domain of moral acceptability (Bar-Tal, 1990). Opotov (1990, p. 1) explains as follows:

> Moral exclusion occurs when individuals or groups are perceived as outside the boundary in which moral values, rules and considerations of fairness apply. Those who are morally excluded are perceived as nonentities, expendable, or undeserving. Consequently, harming or exploiting them appears to be appropriate, acceptable, or just.

Tileaga (2007, p. 721) continues that in order to identify how ontogolisation happens, we need to look at discursive practices. Particular ways of speaking might depersonalise and dehumanise the Other (Billig, 2002), and therefore, looking at examples of public and private discourses about FDHs in Hong Kong might help us understand how they are denied their humanity and hence, become morally excluded.

In her analysis of public discourses about FDHs in Hong Kong, Constable (2007) found that prejudiced, even blatantly racist, comments about this group of people occur frequently in the press. Most notably, their right to occupy public space in the city has been questioned in editorials and letters to the editor. One editorial in the *South China Morning Post*, Hong Kong's major English-language newspaper, pointed out that Filipinos 'are guest workers with no "divine right" to commandeer Central for their own use' (Constable, 2007, p. 4). On Sundays and public holidays, thousands of domestic workers gather in parks and other public venues in Central and on the Kowloon Peninsula to be together, to eat, talk and socialise. This has led to widespread criticism that they have 'invaded' or 'taken over' the public sphere and prevent other people from using it, or they are accused of 'loitering around creating all kinds of nuisance' (p. 5). Note how public discourses construct FDHs as homogenised groups and thus, deprive them of their identity as individuals. As pointed out by Nair-Venugopal (2009, p. 77) 'if individuals are only seen to represent the cultures they belong to, they then cease to be individuals in their own right and become devoid of individual agency'.

If we turn to the private discourses about FDHs, moral exclusion becomes even more apparent. Ladegaard (2011b) asked local Hong Kong students to discuss their attitudes to seven social groups in Hong Kong. In these discussions, Filipina domestic helpers were positioned as 'noisy', 'unfriendly' and 'cunning'; it was argued that 'they go home and get pregnant deliberately so that can quit their job, or they steal' (p. 145), and it was even argued that 'we have to be mean to them or they'll become cocky, and I heard this from my aunt who has a maid' (p. 146). Racist discourses are found everywhere, and the examples uncovered in these Hong Kong students' discussions are not significantly different from many of the examples found in other socio-cultural contexts (e.g. Augoustinos & Every, 2007; Condor, Figgou, Abell, Gibson, & Stevenson, 2006; Ladegaard, 2011a; van Dijk, 1992, 2008; Wetherell & Potter, 1992). However, what is remarkable about these Hong Kong students' private discourses is that there is an apparent lack of hedging and mitigation. No attempts are made to soften the blow of their criticism, and few attempts are made to present positive counter-stereotypes to balance negative ones, which suggests that these discourses may not even be seen as prejudiced. Jost and Banaji (1994, p. 10) argue that stereotypes serve ideological functions in that 'they justify the exploitation of certain groups over others', and because 'they explain the poverty and powerlessness of some groups and the success of others in ways that make these differences seem legitimate and even natural'.

When blatantly racist discourses are left unopposed in group discussions, and when negative outgroup stereotypes about certain groups are not hedged or mitigated, it suggests that such discourses are legitimate and natural. In line with the social constructionist framework that was adopted for this study, we see how ways of talking about certain groups are used to discursively accomplish their depersonalisation and dehumanisation. When FDHs are positioned as robots, or as animals, or inanimate household commodities which may be exchanged like faulty goods, employers are effectively contributing to their depersonalisation and dehumanisation.

In Tileaga's work on the discursive dehumanisation of Romanies (2005, 2007), it is argued that the moral exclusion of this ethnic group implies the 'differentiating power of the absence of national space' (Tileaga, 2007, p. 733). In other words, the ontogolisation of ethnic groups is related to the absence of a space they can call their own. FDHs from the Philippines and Indonesia may have a place they refer to as 'home', but since they live in the diaspora, they do not have access to any space they can legitimately call their own. FDHs are caught between a home country which has been unable to provide for their basic needs and hence, has essentially forced them in to exile, and a host country which refuses to accept them and provide them with a new home. Thus, the only identity available to FDHs is a fractured identity which is tied to, and at the same time separate from, 'home', that is, a diasporic identity which requires them to be engaged in 'compartmentalized forgetting and remembering simultaneously' (Lai, 2011, p. 580). They need to forget 'home' because it is out of reach, and yet, they also need to remember (their families back) home because this provides them with the strength to endure their hardships (Ladegaard, 2012). Tileaga (2007, p. 722) concludes: 'Constructing particular ethnic groups as out-of-place, as transgressing normative place-appropriate conduct, as abject, as repulsive [...], act as symbolic resources for reproducing their delegitimization, their depersonalization (and ultimately their dehumanization).'

In Constable's analysis of the public discourses about FDHs (2007), she found repeated reference to their occupation of public space in Hong Kong as a cause for concern, and the participants in Ladegaard's study complain that Filipino helpers 'always occupy Victoria Park' and 'make [us] unhappy' (2011b, p. 144). The underlying assumption is that they have no right to their own space, and when FDHs are constructed as out of place, or as transgressing place-appropriate conduct, this effectively contributes to their dehumanisation. Vera, a 44-year-old domestic worker from the Philippines, testifies that her employer used to call her 'poor Filipino, stupid Filipino', and subsequently tell her to 'go home', and Maryane's employer in Excerpt 1 tells her to go and kill herself. Thus, FDHs cannot make any claim to space, public or private, in their host country, and their homeland is out of bounds. They are therefore positioned as 'being beyond difference and comparison, beyond the moral order, constituting an "outside" that does not include the possibility of an "inside", that does not include the possibility of shared physical and moral space' (Tileaga, 2005, p. 618).

Conclusion

This paper analysed five excerpts from a large corpus of domestic helper narratives. The examples illustrate how FDHs in Hong Kong are victims of depersonalisation and dehumanisation, and how employers deprive domestic workers of the most fundamental rights, such as eating, resting and sleeping, and talking to and socialising with other FDHs. It was argued that employers' denigration affects FDHs' identity and self-categorisation so that many see themselves as inferior and not worthy of other people's respect. In other words, other-denigration leads to self-denigration, and only when FDHs manage to get away from abusive employers and enjoy the support of other domestic workers may they get empowered to question enforced identities and seek to re-author their own life-stories. It was further argued that positioning FDHs as beyond the moral order paved the way for legitimising exploitation and abuse, and for voicing attitudes with 'eliminationist connotations' (cf. 'you better die', Excerpt 1; see also Tileaga, 2005, p. 619).

The research reported in this paper calls for action from researchers who work with and for FDHs. Threadgold (2005) calls upon researchers not just to analyse the narratives of underprivileged groups, but also to '*rewrite* them in order to change the dominant kinds of social realities and selves (habitus) which they produce' (p. 264). In Threadgold's research on asylum seekers in the UK, this involved influencing the media's representations of these groups, that is, a politics of mixing advocacy with research and knowledge production (see also Phipps, this issue). If predominant stereotypes about FDHs and ideologies of moral exclusion in Hong Kong (and elsewhere) are to be changed, education and information are required. Therefore, researchers need to liaise with voluntary organisations, the press and policymakers, and to achieve this end, domestic helper narratives may be used 'as theory, as practice, as politics and as strategy' (Threadgold, 2005, p. 274).

Acknowledgements

The research reported in the paper was supported by a research grant from the University Grants Committee of Hong Kong. I wish to express my gratitude to the staff and volunteers at the Mission to Migrant Workers, St John's Cathedral, and at the Bethune House shelter for migrant women, in particular, Cynthia Tellez, Edwina Antonio, Juvy Bustamante and Sol Pillar. I am also grateful to Nicola Wong, Junius Santoso and Febby Melissa for their hard work with the transcription and translation of data. Last but not least, I wish to express my sincere gratitude and appreciation to all the FDHs at Bethune House who willingly shared their stories with me and their friends. My admiration for them, for their courage and for the sacrifices they are making for their families, goes far beyond words.

Notes

1. All names of foreign domestic helpers used in this paper are pseudonyms.
2. The concept of depersonalisation has diverse meanings in the literature. In this paper, it is used to imply a milder form of dehumanisation. In his original account of depersonalisation and dehumanisation in intergroup communication, Tajfel (1981) suggested a continuum between the two concepts. Thus, depersonalisation implies that individuals are perceived as group members exclusively leading to loss of individuation and social alienation, and dehumanisation refers to the ultimate depersonalisation where group members are positioned as non-human, or as less than human, which justifies social exclusion.
3. The term 'interviewer' is used in want of a better term. The person who is in charge of a sharing session is not an interviewer in any traditional sense. One of the main objectives of the sharing session is to document the details of a particular case, which means s/he may ask many clarifying questions. Another main objective is to encourage the women to tell their stories, to offer support and advice, and to facilitate a process of empowerment.
4. FDHs in Hong Kong have to pay extortionate agency fees. Indonesian helpers currently pay about HK$21,000, while most Filipinas pay about HK$15,000. The agencies can only charge the helpers 10% of their first month's salary (presently about HK$380), so instead they demand the women attend compulsory training courses before they arrive in Hong Kong for which they have to pay huge fees. The training usually consists of hands-on exercises in mopping floors and doing the dishes, and might be followed by one to two months of 'training' in Hong Kong during which they do housework for the agent, or for his/her family – for free.

References

Augoustinos, M., & Every, D. (2007). Contemporary racist discourse: Taboos against racism and racist accusations. In A. Weatherall, B. Watson, & C. Gallois (Eds.), *Language, discourse and social psychology* (pp. 233–254). Basingstoke: Palgrave Macmillan.

Bar-Tal, D. (1990). Causes and consequences of delegitimization: Models of conflict and ethnocentrism. *Journal of Social Issues, 46,* 65–81.

Benwell, B., & Stokoe, E. (2006). *Discourse and identity.* Edinburgh: Edinburgh University Press.

Billig, M. (2002). Henri Tajfel's cognitive aspects of prejudice and the psychology of bigotry. *British Journal of Social Psychology, 41,* 171–188.

Bloomfield, D. (2000). Voices on the web: Student teachers negotiating identity. *Asia-Pacific Journal of Teacher Education, 28*(3), 199–214.

Brown, C., & Augusta-Scott, T. (Eds.). (2007). *Narrative therapy: Making meaning, making lives.* London: Sage.

Burr, V. (1995). *An introduction to social constructionism.* London: Routledge.

Cameron, D., Fraser, E., Harvey, P., Rampton, M.B.H., & Richardson, K. (1992). *Researching language. Issues of power and method.* London: Routledge.

Caton, S.C. (2010). Abu Ghraib and the problem of evil. In M. Lambek (Ed.), *Ordinary ethics. Anthropology, language, and action* (pp. 165–184). New York: Fordham University Press.

Chiu, S. (2005). *A stranger in the house. Foreign domestic helpers in Hong Kong.* Hong Kong: Hong Kong Institute of Asia-Pacific Studies & the Chinese University of Hong Kong.

Condor, S., Figgou, L., Abell, J., Gibson, S., & Stevenson, C. (2006). 'They're not racist …' Prejudice denial, mitigation and suppression in dialogue. *British Journal of Social Psychology, 45*, 441–462.

Constable, N. (1997). Sexuality and discipline among Filipina domestic workers in Hong Kong. *American Ethnologist, 24*(3), 539–558.

Constable, N. (2007). *Maid to order in Hong Kong. Stories of migrant workers* (2nd ed.). Ithaca, NY: Cornell University Press.

Cortazzi, M. (2001). Narrative analysis in ethnography. In P. Atkinson, A. Coffey, S. Delamont, J. Lofland, & L. Lofland (Eds.), *Handbook of ethnography* (pp. 384–394). London: Sage.

De Fina, A. (2006). Group identity, narrative and self-representations. In A. De Fina, D. Schiffrin, & M. Bamberg (Eds.), *Discourse and identity* (pp. 351–375). Cambridge: Cambridge University Press.

De Fina, A., & Baynham, M. (2005). Introduction: Dislocations/relocations. Narratives of displacement. In M. Baynham & A. De Fina (Eds.), *Dislocations/relocations. Narratives of displacement* (pp. 1–14). Manchester: St Jerome.

Duvall, J., & Béres, L. (2007). Movements of identities. A map for therapeutic conversations about trauma. In C. Brown & T. Augusta-Scott (Eds.), *Narrative therapy: Making meaning, making lives* (pp. 229–259). London: Sage.

Holmes, J. (2006). *Gendered talk at work. Constructing gender identity through workplace discourse.* Oxford: Blackwell.

Holmes, J., & Marra, M. (2002). Humour as a discursive boundary marker in social interaction. In A. Duszak (Ed.), *Us and others. Social identities across languages, discourses and cultures* (pp. 377–400). Amsterdam: John Benjamins.

Jackson, R.L., & Moshin, J. (2010). Identity and difference: Race and the necessity of the discriminating subject. In T.K. Nakayama & R.T. Halualani (Eds.), *The handbook of critical intercultural communication* (pp. 348–363). Oxford: Wiley-Blackwell.

Jost, J.T., & Banaji, M.R. (1994). The role of stereotyping in system-justification and the production of false consciousness. *British Journal of Social Psychology, 33*, 1–27.

Ladegaard, H.J. (2011a). Stereotypes and the discursive accomplishment of intergroup differentiation: Talking about 'the other' in a global business organization. *Pragmatics, 21*(1), 85–109.

Ladegaard, H.J. (2011b). Stereotypes in the making: Prejudice and cultural generalizations in Hong Kong students' discourse. *Journal of Asian Pacific Communication, 21*(1), 133–158.

Ladegaard, H.J. (2012). The discourse of powerlessness and repression: Identity construction in domestic helper narratives. *Journal of Sociolinguistics, 16*(4), 450–482.

Ladegaard, H.J. (in press). Laughing at adversity: Laughter as communication in domestic helper narratives.

Lai, M.Y. (2011). The present of forgetting: Diasporic identity and migrant domestic workers in Hong Kong. *Social Identities, 17*(4), 565–585.

Medved, M.I., & Brockmeier, J. (2008). Talking about the unthinkable. Neurotrama and the 'catastrophic reaction. In L.C. Hydén & J. Brockmeier (Eds.), *Health, illness and culture: Broken narratives* (pp. 52–72). New York: Routledge.

Nair-Venugopal, S. (2009). Interculturalities: Reframing identities in intercultural communication. *Language and Intercultural Communication, 9*(2), 76–90.

Opotov, S. (1990). Moral exclusion and injustice: An introduction. *Journal of Social Issues, 46*(1), 1–20.

Payne, M. (2006). *Narrative therapy* (2nd ed.). London: Sage.

Riessman, C.K. (2003). Performing identities in illness narratives: Masculinity and multiple sclerosis. *Qualitative Research, 3*(1), 5–33.

Sampson, E. (1993). *Celebrating the other: A dialogic account of human nature.* Boulder, CO: Westview Press.

Saville-Troike, M. (2003). *The ethnography of communication* (3rd ed.). Oxford: Blackwell.

Shuman, A. (2005). *Other people's stories: Entitlement claims and the critique of empathy.* Urbana: University of Illinois Press.

Solis, J. (2004). Narrating and counternarrating illegality as an identity. In C. Daiute & C. Lightfoot (Eds.), *Narrative analysis. Studying the development of individuals in society* (pp. 181–199). London: Sage.

Tajfel, H. (1981). *Human groups and social categories: Studies in social psychology.* Cambridge: Cambridge University Press.

Taylor, C. (1994). The politics of recognition. In A. Gutmann (Ed.), *Multiculturalism. Examining the politics of recognition* (pp. 25–73). Princeton, NJ: Princeton University Press.

Threadgold, T. (2005). Performing theories of narrative. Theorising narrative performance. In J. Thornborrow & J. Coates (Eds.), *The sociolinguistics of narrative* (pp. 261–278). Amsterdam: John Benjamins.

Thurlow, C. (2010). Speaking of difference: Language, inequality and interculturality. In T.K. Nakayama & R.T. Halualani (Eds.), *The handbook of critical intercultural communication* (pp. 227–247). Oxford: Wiley-Blackwell.

Tileaga, C. (2005). Accounting for extreme prejudice and legitimating blame in talk about the Romanies. *Discourse & Society, 16*(5), 603–624.

Tileaga, C. (2007). Ideologies of moral exclusion: A critical discursive reframing of depersonalization, delegitimization and dehumanization. *British Journal of Social Psychology, 46,* 717–737.

Toolan, M. (2001). *Narrative analysis. A critical linguistic introduction* (2nd ed.). London: Routledge.

Van Dijk, T. (1992). Discourse and the denial of racism. *Discourse & Society, 3*(1), 87–118.

Van Dijk, T. (2008). *Discourse and power.* Basingstoke: Palgrave Macmillan.

Verkuyten, M. (2001). 'Abnormalization' of ethnic minorities in conversation. *British Journal of Social Psychology, 40,* 257–278.

Wetherell, M., & Potter, J. (1992). *Mapping the language of racism. Discourse and the legitimation of exploitation.* Hemel Hempstead: Harvester Wheatsheaf.

Zimbardo, P. (2007). *The Lucifer effect. Understanding how good people turn evil.* New York: Random House.

Appendix. Notes on transcription

Transcription conventions
Bold=pronounced with stress/emphasis
[it's a]=words inserted by the transcriber to make sense
,=short pause, less than 0.5 second
(2.0)=pause in seconds
'give me that'=reporting direct speech
: (as in ah:)=means that the vowel sound is prolonged
xx=incomprehensible
//=interruption
//as I said//=overlapping speech.

Issues of language choice, ethics and equity: Japanese retirees living in Malaysia as their second home

Siti Hamin Stapa[a], Talaibek Musaev[b], Natsue Hieda[a] and Normalis Amzah[a]

[a]Faculty of Social Sciences and Humanities, The National University of Malaysia, Selangor, Malaysia; [b]Faculty of Languages and Linguistics, University of Malaya, Kuala Lumpur, Malaysia

This paper will discuss two issues related to Japanese retirees adopting Malaysia as their second home. The first is that of the preferred language choice of the retirees. To collect data for language choice a self-report questionnaire was administered and an interview was conducted. The findings suggest that the majority of the retirees chose English for both informal and formal interactions in Malaysia. It may be inferred that they are not motivated to learn the local language although quite clearly that would facilitate intercultural communication with the locals. Based on these findings we examine the ethical considerations underlying their language preferences. We assume that they have positioned themselves as sojourners who have come to reside in Malaysia principally to enjoy their retirement, rather than as settlers. We have named this unique situation – *contemplation* – based on an observation of their emotional adaptation to the new environment since their personal needs are taken care of by Japanese agents or by locating a 'little Japan' in Malaysia for themselves. The MM2H programme hosted by the Malaysian government focuses on economic aspects of the partnership and does not seek to provide intercultural opportunities or benefits which implicate issues of ethics and equity.

Kertas kerja ini akan membincangkan dua isu berkaitan pesara Jepun yang memilih Malaysia sebagai rumah kedua mereka. Isu yang pertama adalah tentang bahasa pilihan pesara ini sewaktu menetap di Malaysia. Data telah diperolehi melalui satu soal selidik dan laporan kendiri. Dapatan menunjukkan bahawa majoriti pesara memilih bahasa Inggeris untuk berinteraksi dalam keadaan rasmi dan tidak rasmi. Ini memberi tanggapan bahawa mereka tidak mempunyai motivasi untuk mempelajari bahasa tempatan yang sepatutnya boleh menggalak-kan mereka berkomunikasi dengan orang tempatan. Berdasarkan dapatan ini kami melihat isu berkaitan dengan pertimbangan etika disebalik pemilihan bahasa mereka. Kami menganggap bahawa mereka telah meletakkan diri mereka sebagai pendatang yang datang ke Malaysia semata-mata untuk menikmati persaraan mereka. Situasi yang unik ini kami namakan sebagai – *kontemplasi* – berdasarkan pengamatan mengenai adaptasi emosi mereka terhadap persekitaran yang baru kerana semua keperluan mereka dijaga oleh ejen-ejen Jepun atau melalui 'penempatan masyarakat Jepun' di Malaysia. Program MM2H di bawah naungan kerajaan Malaysia sebenarnya berfokus kepada aspek berkerjasama dalam bidang ekonomi bukan bertujuan memberi peluang dalam aspek silang atau antarbudaya yang berimplikasi isu etika dan equiti.

Introduction

The phenomenon of retirees migrating to a new country is not something that only began in the recent past. This has been taking place as early as the 1970s in Northern Europe where retirees from the UK and Germany migrated to areas near the Mediterranean Sea (King, Warnes, & Williams, 2000). Migration does not have a singular pattern but criss-crosses boundaries and demography. According to the AON (2010) report, many retirees from Western and Northern Europe favour a warmer country such as Spain. More specifically, the report indicates that 58% of respondents from the UK, 54% from Germany and 47% from Switzerland desire migrating to another country.

The history of Japanese retirees migrating to a new country, however, is not as old as that of Europe's. Beginning from the end of the nineteenth century until the 1970s, most of the Japanese retirees who migrated did so for economic reasons. They emigrated mostly to Brazil and Hawaii. However, in the recent past and today, most middle-class Japanese migrate not so much for economic reasons but for other reasons (Ip, Wu, & Inglis, 1998). This new phenomenon is termed *lifestyle migration* vis-à-vis the *labour migration* of an earlier time (Sato, 2001). According to Kubo and Ishikawa (2004), Japanese retirees migrate for reasons such as a more comfortable living environment, lower prices of goods and services, and self-satisfaction within a new lifestyle. This could be attributed to worries about economic unpredictability, social responsibility and uncertain feelings about their lives in Japan. The political stability and economic growth of Malaysia has been cited as the main draw together with the absence of major disasters (*Star*, 15 June 2012). In addition to that, the Look East Policy, which was introduced in 1981 as a government plan to look less to the West and more to Japan (Lim, 1984) for economic leadership, had helped to build a cordial relationship between the two countries making living here more convenient and conducive for the Japanese.

Charles Taylor (1994) argues that all societies are increasingly becoming multicultural and are more open to multicultural migration. Being a middle-income country (World Bank, 2011), Malaysia is particularly strategic for migration due to its accessibility to people from developed countries and the rich from developing countries. The government of Malaysia introduced the Silver Hair Programme (later renamed Malaysia My Second Home) to promote Malaysia as a prime destination for foreign retirees looking for a second home. The Malaysia My Second Home programme (abbreviated to MM2H) is an international residency scheme enacted by the Government of Malaysia to allow foreigners to live in the country on a long-stay visa of up to 10 years. To qualify for the programme, applicants must meet certain financial and medical criteria. Successful applicants are then entitled to enter and leave the country on a largely unrestricted basis while benefitting from other incentives aimed at making their stay in Malaysia more attractive.

This programme has attracted many Japanese retirees to settle down in Malaysia. This paper reports on the language choices of such Japanese adopting Malaysia as their second home. It also examines some of the ethical considerations underlying their choices. Language choice is considered significant as the retirees have the choice of learning the local language or relying on English, which is the second widely spoken language particularly in the urban areas in Malaysia. While residing in a host country (it is assumed) it would be ethical to learn and use the local language so as to be part of the community; to be welcomed by the local people and to interact with them. However, as English is widely used in Malaysia they have the choice of either learning the local language or relying on English for communication purposes within the country. It would be interesting to investigate their choice of language for interpersonal communication with the locals.

'Malaysia My Second Home'

The Malaysia My Second Home (MM2H) programme has been promoted by the Malaysian government to allow individuals from all over the world who fulfil certain criteria to stay for long periods in Malaysia on a social visit pass with a multiple entry visa. It is open to citizens of countries recognized by Malaysia, regardless of race, religion, gender or age. The programme allows applicants to be accompanied by their spouses, parents and children. Foreign spouses of Malaysians and expatriates who wish to retire in Malaysia after the expiration of their employment passes are also eligible to apply to stay in Malaysia under this programme.

Applicants can be accompanied by their spouses, unmarried children below the age of 21 and parents above the age of 60 as dependants. There were 13,998 approved cases from 2003 to 2010. Thus, the MM2H programme has come a long way from its predecessor, the Silver Hair Programme, which only approved 828 cases from 1996 to 2000. This improvement could be attributed to the efficiency of the authorities involved, notably the Ministry of Tourism and the Immigration Department, which have taken proactive steps to implement numerous incentives, such as setting up a One-stop Centre, increasing publicity and cultivating a pool of licensed agents to act as on-the-ground salesmen for the programme.

Indeed the target market has grown large enough for clients to be segmented into three broad categories. The first category includes middle-income people from rich countries who hope to stretch their retirement funds further in Malaysia, attracted by its lower living costs along with reasonable living standards. The second category comprises the rich from poorer countries attracted by the comparatively higher living standards and credible amenities in Malaysia for education and health care. The third category includes expatriates who have worked in Malaysia, become comfortable living in the region and have decided to stay on in Malaysia upon retirement. Government authorities recently encouraged the growth of an additional segment to make it possible for expatriates working in Malaysia to enter seamlessly into the MM2H programme after they have completed their tenure of service.

Foreigners consider many factors when choosing to live in another country. Among these are prices and the ease of ownership of properties, cost of living, health care benefits and security. Malaysia competes with other countries that provide retirement schemes too. So far, the MM2H scheme has been generating good ratings compared to those of other countries. Simultaneously, in trying to maintain those ratings, the government is projecting Malaysia as a 'safe easy access' place. Ono (2008, p. 154) states that the MM2H programme aims to increase income from tourism and stimulate the economy through active foreign investment and the acquisition of foreign currency.

One of the advantages of living in Malaysia is the low cost of living due to the favourable currency exchange rate with many other currencies. MM2H participants can stretch their dollar, pound, yen, riyal or dirham further without much of a sacrifice in standards of living. In 2008, the Swiss Bank UBS surveyed 71 comparable cities in the world from London to Jakarta. Kuala Lumpur was rated the cheapest place to buy an identical basket of 122 goods (see Malaysia My Second Home website: http://www.mm2h.gov.my/col.php).

In February 2009, the Malaysian government authorities came up with several new incentives to promote the MM2H programme to a wider world market. These new incentives included the possibility that participants can engage in active businesses, work up to 20 hours a week and that their children can be dependants up until 21 years of age. Foreign spouses of Malaysians, expatriates in Malaysia and parents of the main applicant, are all eligible to participate in the programme. MM2H ID Cards have been made available to them as well. These incentives coupled with provisions allowing foreigners to own property with no inheritance tax, no taxation on income repatriated from overseas and no real property tax prove to be very attractive to foreigners looking for a second home.

The number of participants for this programme has increased due to the incentives mentioned above. Table 1 shows the number of participants from 2006 to 2013.

We can see that the MM2H programme has attracted many foreigners to Malaysia including participants from Japan. Table 1 indicates that participants from Japan who were number four in 2006 had moved to number one compared to those from other countries for the years 2011 and 2012.

Methodology

Since the objective of the study was to investigate language choice for interaction (apart from their mother tongue, Japanese) and to understand cultural behaviour within the cross-cultural environment of Japanese participants of the MM2H programme, the first step in data collection was to identify the Japanese participants of the study. The total number of participants of the survey was 120 Japanese citizens; 50.8% of them were males and 48.3% females. Their ages ranged from 40 to above 80 years. The percentages of their ages are: 40–49 (1.7%), 50–59 (16.7%), 60–69 (64.2%), 70–79 (13.3%), and 80 and above (1.7%). This shows that the majority of the survey respondents are between 60 and 69 years old. Generally, people retire at this age. Their educational qualifications are as follows: elementary/junior high school (3.3%), followed by high school (31.7%) and vocational school

Table 1.   Top 10 countries from 2006 to 2012.

Rank	2006	2007	2008	2009	2010	2011	2012 (March)
1	Bangladesh	UK	Iran	Iran	Iran	Japan	Japan
2	China	Japan	Japan	Japan	Japan	China	China
3	UK	Korea	UK	UK	China	Iran	Bangladesh
4	Japan	Bangladesh	China	China	UK	Bangladesh	Iran
5	Singapore	China	Korea	Pakistan	Pakistan	UK	UK
6	USA	Sri Lanka	Bangladesh	Bangladesh	Bangladesh	Pakistan	Australia
7	Korea	Iran	Pakistan	Australia	Singapore	Singapore	Pakistan
8	Indonesia	Singapore	Sri Lanka	Singapore	Australia	Australia	Korea
9	Taiwan	USA	Singapore	Korea	India	Taiwan	Taiwan
10	Australia	Australia	USA	Indonesia	Korea	Korea	Singapore

Source: Malaysia My Second Home programme: http://www.mm2h.gov.my

(10.0%). A total of 12.5% are diploma holders, 40.0% are degree holders, while 0.8% have a doctorate degree. The most common occupations are company workers (35.0%) followed by housewives (37%). The remaining participants are professionals (5.8%), government servants (6.7%), self-employed workers (13.3%), part-time workers (3.3%) and unspecified others (2.5%).

We developed a self-report questionnaire for the study and managed to pilot test the questionnaire at the Japan Club in Kuala Lumpur. The questionnaire was written up in Japanese to make it easier for the participants to understand the questions and provide responses. It was divided into sections: the background of the respondents, perceptions of living conditions in Malaysia, interpersonal communication and language use. Based on the feedback we received from the pilot test, we revised the questionnaire before administering it to the participants. We managed to contact the President of the Second Home Club. With the assistance provided by the President, we administered the questionnaire to those residing in Kuala Lumpur and outer Kuala Lumpur (the Klang Valley). The President of the Second Home Club introduced us later to the President of the Tropical Resort Lifestyle Company, and through him, we administered the questionnaire to the participants residing on the island of Penang.

The second instrument for this research was an informal interview. Five participants were randomly selected to take part in it. The purpose of conducting the interview was to support findings from the questionnaire. Although they were randomly selected, interviewees were from diverse backgrounds in terms of areas of residence, gender and length of stay in Malaysia. Three males and two females residing in Kuala Lumpur and Cameron Highlands (200 km north of Kuala Lumpur) with the length of their stays ranging from 2 to 10 years were selected.

Findings

Language exposure

In order to discuss language choice for the daily communication needs of the Japanese retirees, we first looked at their exposure to foreign languages, that is, English and Malay. Data from the questionnaire survey revealed that the retirees had learned both English and Malay for a certain period of time. Figure 1 shows the length of study for both languages.

As shown in Figure 1, a greater number of participants learned English rather than Malay. A majority learned English for six months and above but the highest percentage is of participants who learned the language for more than four years. This is particularly true as English is taught in schools in Japan. On the other hand, the length of study for of participants who learned Malay was less than three months.

Figure 2 presents the level of language proficiency among the MM2H participants. As we can see, most of the participants are not very proficient in either English or Malay. The majority of participants seem to have acquired only a basic level of proficiency in English. Similarly, the majority of participants have a low proficiency level in Malay.

The following section will discuss findings from the questionnaire survey through which the respondents were asked to indicate their choice of language for different communicative purposes. The dominant languages used in Malaysia are Malay,

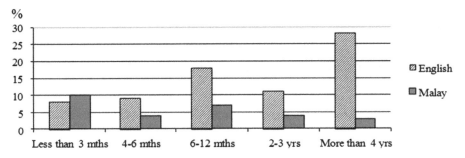

Figure 1.   Length of participants' language study.

Chinese and Tamil with English as the second language. Most urban Malaysians speak at least two languages, their mother tongue and a second language, if not more.

The language choice of the respondents will be discussed based on the following situations: non-formal (greetings, self-introductions, etc.), formal (making complaints, explaining illness to a doctor, conducting banking transactions, etc.), and use of the media (newspapers, TV, radio) and the Internet. The findings of the study will be reported based on frequency (number of respondents out of 120 who had responded to the questions) and percentage (as a portion of 100%). For the discussion of the findings, we will use the following codes for the language choices: English (1), Malay (2), Chinese (3) and Tamil (4).

Language choice: non-formal situations

The discussion for the non-formal situation begins with the choice of language for self-introductions, greetings, shopping, asking for directions and talking to local friends. The percentages shown in the findings are related to: English (1), Malay (2), Chinese (3) and Tamil (4), with the remainder of the total percentage being Japanese language use. The findings are presented in Table 2.

The results of the survey reveal that more than half of the respondents (68.3%) chose English for self-introductions followed by a combination choice of both English and Malay (13.3%). For the purpose of greetings, a similar language preference was evident with just over half of the respondents (55.0%) choosing

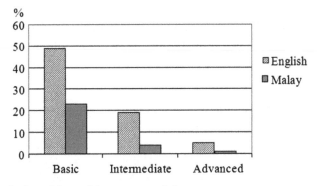

Figure 2.   Level of participants' language proficiency.

Table 2. Non-formal situations.

	Language	Frequency	Percentage
SELF-INTRODUCTIONS	1	82	68.3
	1, 2	16	13.3
	1, 3	1	0.8
	2	3	2.5
	1, 2, 3	1	0.8
GREETINGS	1	66	55.0
	1, 2	32	26.7
	1, 2, 3	9	7.5
	1, 3	1	0.8
	1, 2, 4	1	0.8
	2	2	1.7
SHOPPING	1	81	67.5
	1, 2	21	17.5
	1, 3	1	0.8
	2	6	5.0
ASKING FOR DIRECTIONS	1	79	65.8
	1, 2	9	7.5
	1, 3	1	0.8
	2	2	1.7
TALKING WITH LOCAL FRIENDS	1	63	52.5
	1, 2	7	5.8
	1, 3	1	0.8
	2	1	0.8
	3	1	0.8

1 = English; 2 = Malay; 3 = Chinese; 4 = Tamil.

the English language. Those who used English and Malay follow this with a percentage of 26.7%. Only nine respondents (7.5%) reported that they used three languages: English, Malay and Chinese. Only one used Tamil because it was unknown to the other respondents.

A majority of the respondents (67.5%) chose to communicate in English with others while shopping. This was followed by the choice of both English and Malay (17.5%). A similar pattern was indicated in asking for directions with English as the first choice for 79 of the 120 respondents (65.8%) and the second choice was for both English and Malay (7.5%).

In coping with the demands of daily life in Malaysia, the Japanese participants need to communicate with their local friends. Most of the respondents chose English (52.5%) for this purpose, while 5.8% used both English and Malay.

Language choice: formal situations

This section discusses the language preferred by the participants in formal situations, beginning with banking transactions or post office transactions, followed by explanations of an illness to a doctor, booking hotel accommodation and airline tickets, dealing with bureaucratic procedures and for making complaints. The findings are summarized in Table 3.

Table 3. Formal situations.

	Language	Frequency	Percentage
BANKING/POST OFFICE TRANSACTIONS	1	79	65.8
	1, 2	4	3.3
	2	4	3.3
EXPLAINING SICKNESS TO A DOCTOR	1	61	50.8
	1, 2	2	1.7
	2	1	0.8
	3	1	0.8
AIRLINE TICKET AND HOTEL RESERVATIONS	1	74	61.7
	1, 2	3	2.5
	1, 3	1	0.8
CONDUCTING BUREAUCRATIC PROCEDURES	1	51	42.5
	1, 2	3	2.5
	2	2	1.7
MAKING COMPLAINTS	1	48	40.0
	1, 2	2	1.7
	2	3	2.5
	3	1	0.8

1 = English; 2 = Malay; 3 = Chinese; 4 = Tamil.

The Japanese MM2H respondents preferred to use English (65.8%) during transactions in a bank or post office. A similar use of English (50.8%) can be seen when explaining symptoms of illnesses to their doctors.

We also asked for their language preferences for booking airline tickets or for making hotel reservations. The results revealed that most participants preferred to use English (61.7%), followed by the use of both English and Malay (2.5%). English was still the dominant language but the participants chose Japanese to make bookings for hotels or airline tickets whenever there was an opportunity to use Japanese. Respondents were also asked about their language preferences if they needed to inquire about procedures at a bureaucratic level, such as dealing with Malaysian government officials. The results are as follows: 42.5% would use English, 2.5% English and Malay, and 1.7% would use Malay. For making complaints, the dominant language was still English (40.0%), Malay (2.5%), and English and Malay (1.7%).

Language choice: use of the media

The final part of this paper discusses language preferences for reading books, magazines and newspapers, listening to the radio and watching television, as well as using the Internet. The findings of the study are presented in Table 4.

The percentage of respondents who preferred to read newspapers/books/ magazines in English is 30.8%. Obviously, most respondents read materials in Japanese for pleasure because using the mother tongue would probably be the most comfortable choice for the respondents in a non-interpersonal situation. They can obtain materials in Japanese from the Japan Foundation library and the Japan Club in Kuala Lumpur. Materials in Japanese are not readily available at local bookshops and news-stands.

Table 4. Use of the media.

	Language	Frequency	Percentage
READING NEWSPAPERS/BOOKS/MAGAZINES	1	37	30.8
	1, 2	1	0.8
	1, 3	1	0.8
	2	1	0.8
	3	1	0.8
LISTENING TO RADIO/WATCHING TV	1	37	30.8
	1, 2	5	4.2
	2	2	1.7
	3	1	0.8
USING INTERNET TO COMPOSE LETTERS/EMAIL	1	44	36.7
	1, 2	1	0.8
	1, 3	1	0.8
	2	1	0.8
USING INTERNET TO FIND INFOMATION	1	37	30.8

1 = English; 2 = Malay; 3 = Chinese; 4 = Tamil.

A total of 30.8% of the respondents preferred to listen to the radio or watch TV in the English language. They also watch Japanese programmes which are available in Malaysia via cable network TV, and listen to Japanese radio programmes which can also be received in Malaysia.

We were also interested in investigating the participants' choice of language for the Internet. A total of 30.8% claimed that they used English for emails. However, more than half did not respond to the question on using the Internet to seek information. As retirees they may not have much interest in searching for information or entertainment on the Internet. It is also assumed that if they needed to, the participants would prefer to choose Japanese whenever there are opportunities to do so.

Discussion

Studies in language choice

Language choice is determined by many factors, such as a speaker's first language, the dominant and community language, age, education, role relationships, ethnicity, social status, and the economic and political position of the linguistic group speakers belong to as well as the neutrality of the language (Dumanig, 2007) in question. The choice of the first language (L1) as a medium of communication among bilingual and multilingual speakers seems to be common in many multilingual societies. Fasold (1990) believes that there is a preference for the first language when speakers are confused as to which language is to be used in certain situations. Speakers tend to prefer their L1 because of familiarity and fluency in the language. The more familiar and fluent the speakers are in their own language, the more convenience and ease is experienced since no extra effort is required to use it. Choosing the first language is not only influenced by convenience and comfort but it also displays one's ethnic identity and language loyalty (Spolsky, 2004).

On the other hand, bilingual and multilingual speakers sometimes prefer using a community language rather than the first language for practical, political and economic reasons. Community languages are languages spoken by members of minority groups or communities within a majority language context. It is widely understood by the entire community. It is easier to use for communicating with others and in transacting business because of language familiarity. Most bilingual and multilingual speakers prefer a community language as their base language as it provides them with more opportunities for economic benefits (Bradley & Bradley, 2002; Degefa, 2004; Johansson, 1991; Yau, 1997).

In some cases, bilingual or multilingual speakers prefer to use the dominant language instead of the community language because of its predominance and prestige in the community (Ferrer & Sankoff, 2004). The use of a more prestigious or dominant language helps speakers to elevate their status in the society. At present, English is regarded as a dominant language in Malaysia just as it is in countries such as Singapore, the Philippines and India to name just a few. Since a dominant language possesses a high status in the community, multilingual speakers tend to choose it because it also provides opportunities for economic benefits (Bradley & Bradley, 2002).

Age is also an influential factor in language choice as people of different age groups vary in their language preferences. Older members of a community may prefer a different language compared to younger members due to differences in language exposure and orientation. In the well-known study conducted on language choices of the Hungarian community in Obertwart, Austria, young people preferred German when speaking with their peers, but used Hungarian when speaking with older members of the community (Gal, 1979). Gal's finding is further supported by Li Wei. Summarizing language choice and language shift among members of the Tyneside Chinese community, he states that '[A] number of extra-linguistic factors have been examined and it has been found that age is the most significant factor associated with this change in language choice and language ability' (Li Wei, 1994, p. 114) towards the use of English.

Rodriguez, Fernandez-Mayoralas, and Rojo (1998) claim that the problems of British retirees in Costa del Sol are difficulties in acquiring the local language. There is not much interest in learning the local language, because people do not need it for most aspects of their everyday lives (Rodriguez et al., 1998, p. 194). Ahmed (2011) supports the findings of Rodriguez et al. (1998) in a study of women retirees in Costa Blanca, Spain. These British cases are similar to those of the MM2H participants with the majority above 60 for whom it was unnecessary to learn a new language. The average age of Ahmed's participants was 62 years and he concludes that one of the factors hindering the participants' learning of Spanish is age (2011). The Japanese MM2H participants have a very efficient support system so they can rely solely on the Japanese language to interact with their fellow Japanese and rely on English to interact with locals. Furthermore, they reside in the urban areas of Malaysia where English is widely spoken. One of the participants wanted to practice the Malay language (she has attended Malay classes) but found it very difficult to do so as all her neighbours spoke to her in English.

The choice of a country to reside in is also determined by the languages spoken. Nagatomo (2007) reported that the main reason the Japanese chose Australia is because English is the primary language spoken there. This is supported by Ono (2008) who claims that Japanese participants are comfortable communicating in English with the locals in Penang, the northern island state of Malaysia. It is interesting to make comparisons with the long-stay Japanese participants in

Thailand. According to Kawahara (2010), in Chiangmai, the Japanese practically do not use English or Thai. English is not widely spoken by the majority of Thai and study of the Thai language by the Japanese seems very difficult for reasons of age-related memory recall and difficulties in pronunciation.

Many retirees from Northern Europe (Rodriguez et al., 1998; Warnes, King, Williams, & Patterson, 1999) as well as from Japan (Stapa, Amzah, Hieda, & Musaev, 2010) say that the most attractive reason for staying in a second home country is a climate that improves and contributes to the enjoyment of a better quality of life. Cultural and linguistic aspects are lower priorities and thus, explain the Japanese participants' 'unwillingness' to integrate with the local community.

Language choice of the Japanese retirees

The study aims to investigate participants' language choice in handling everyday conversations both in formal and informal situations. This paper explores the sociolinguistic practices of Japanese retirees as members of a minority language community in Malaysia who have participated in the Malaysia as My Second Home programme. The findings of the study indicate participants' strong preference for English as the medium of communication with others. The English language is widely spoken in Malaysia and plays an important role in the personal advancement of the individual and in national progress (Foo & Richards, 2004; Kaur, 1995). The Japanese retirees use English since this is the only foreign language that is common among Malaysians. According to Powell and Hashim (2011), although English has no legal status in Malaysia, it is designated to be the 'second most important language'. English is used in many domains by many people, surpassed only by the Malay language. English has remained as the normative language of corporate business in Malaysia too, 'largely because of the legacy of use in colonial British enterprise and traditional links with the English-speaking world' (Nair-Venugopal, 2001, pp. 21–22).

Therefore, in the case of Malaysia, most people, especially in urban areas, speak English quite well, and such areas are where most of the participants of this study currently reside in. Living in urban areas shapes the language choices of the participants because in such areas they can always communicate in English in both formal and informal situations. Furthermore, the fact that the participants are not able to speak other languages like Malay, Chinese or Tamil is another reason for their preference for English. Moreover, participants studied English in school in Japan and one of the reasons for choosing to reside in Malaysia was because English is widely spoken here, making it easier for them to live among Malaysians.

Another factor influencing their choice of language is their age. As discussed earlier, age may be a strong factor in language choice because people of different ages vary in their language preferences (Ahmed, 2011; Gal, 1979; Li Wei, 1994; Rodriguez et al., 1998). The older members of a community may prefer a different language compared to the younger ones due to differences in language exposure and orientation. The majority of the MM2H participants are of retirement age (60 and above) and they do not seem to be motivated to learn a new foreign language for communication purposes when they can use English instead. Ono (2008) asserts that Japanese participants are comfortable using English to interact with local Malaysians.

Issues of culture, ethics and equity in retiree choice

In dealing with issues of culture, ethics and equity, we observe that in addition to English, there are some attempts to use the local languages. In non-formal settings, local languages are used especially for self-introductions, greetings and while shopping. It is assumed that these kinds of efforts somehow contribute to friendlier responses and an amiable atmosphere during the communicative process (Stephanenko, 2004). Language interaction is the main source of social and cultural progress in intercultural relations. Increased stimulation of cultural and information links through learning the local language may lead to more frequent and deeper contacts with the locals, which in turn develops extensive understanding of the surrounding cultural environment. Gradually, successful relationships with the locals result in building up different levels of trust. Thus, despite the widespread use of English in daily life in Malaysia, the role of the English language 'for international rather than intra-national purposes – more a foreign language than a second language' (Crystal, 2003, p. 57), leads us to think that the visible transformation of English as an international medium of communication becomes some kind of barrier that prevents deeper contact with the locals whose languages are more commonly used in daily activities. Moreover, the findings of the survey also revealed that most of the participants reported that their level of English was at the beginner's level (refer to Figure 2). With their limited English language ability they may encounter difficulties in communicating in English too with the locals.

However, if participants are not able to communicate in the local language at a sufficient level of ability with the local people from different backgrounds, regardless of how close the relationships are, there will be some apprehension associated with their ethical principles. The problem of ethics arises from a lack of language competence that may result in the emergence of a barrier between the participants and local groups gradually generating superficial perceptions of the local cultural environment (Stephanenko, 2004). Retirees who have local friends will have a better chance of adapting to the local language and acquire the unwritten rules within the new cultural context, which means greater opportunities to learn about the ethical aspects of cultural relations. The social exchange theory of Thibaut and Kelly (1959) focuses on the rational valuation of self-interest in human relationships where people try to minimize costs while maximizing benefits. This is further supported by Chibocos, Leite, and Weis (2005, p. 137) who state that:

> social exchange theory builds on the assumption that those engaged in interactions are rationally seeking to maximize the profits or benefits to be gained from those situations, especially in terms of meeting basic individual needs. Social exchange theory assumes that social exchanges between or among two or more individuals are efforts by participants to fulfill basic needs.

On the other hand, equity theory (Walster, Walster, & Bersheid, 1978) proposes that relationship outcomes are based upon what participants contribute to the relationship in proportion to what they obtain from them, or how to evaluate justly or fairly the distribution of costs and benefits for each partner.

MM2H participants, who have developed their lifestyles in one cultural context, are now attempting to live in a new cultural context. Do they continue to act in the new setting as they did in the previous one, or do they change their behaviours to more appropriate ones to the new setting? Nair-Venugopal (2003, p. 40) makes the interesting point that, 'where both participants and locals are non-native speakers of English, the communication process at least will proceed unhindered by perceived intentions to exert power through linguistic hegemony'. When the participants and local counterparts do not experience psychological pressure from the 'correctness' of 'language competence, emotions and of course, cultural habits, both sides realize that they stand to gain if they are able to communicate successfully to close mutually beneficial business deals in a win-win situation' (ibid.). Correspondingly, Phillipson (2003) argues that from a communicative point of view, as well as from the point of language equity, there is a problem of communication when you cannot expect a non-native speaker to fully advance the subtleties of a foreign language, and thus, communication between native and non-native speakers will always be asymmetrical. On the other hand, in the process of communication where counterparts are non-native speakers, then this kind of asymmetry is eliminated, revealing the surface of the neutrality of the language and thus making communication comfortable for both parties. However, if they are communicating with native speakers, then there may be a kind of language pressure on them during conversations due to the fact that incorrect pronunciation is often dismissed as unintelligent by native speakers (Phillipson, 2003). This can be attested to with reference to the retirees in the MM2H programme. Participants who developed their English language competence in one cultural context succeeded in adapting it to the new context of their resettlement. In their choice of Malaysia for settlement, they feel they are of equal status with Malaysians in the use of English since both (the Japanese retirees and the locals) are non-native speakers.

Japanese retirees who come from a 'generally mono-cultural, mono-lingual nation' (Koike, 1993, pp. 277–278), would expect some kind of 'unexpected situations' living in multicultural and multilingual Malaysia which is very different from where they come from. According to Oberg (1960), who introduced the term *cultural shock*, the 'shock' starts from the idea that entering into a new cultural context is accompanied by unpleasant feelings such as the loss of friends and status, rejection, surprise and discomfort in the knowledge of the differences between cultures, as well as confusion in value orientation, social and personal behaviour. Berry (1997) points out that the term 'acculturation' is employed to refer to the cultural changes resulting from group encounters involved in cross-cultural exchanges; while 'shock' is associated only with negative experiences. Acculturation can be shown in intercultural contact to be a positive experience via an assessment of problems and in overcoming them. Berry (1997) has identified four aspects for the concept of acculturation, namely: assimilation, separation, integration and marginalization. As can be seen in the case of the MM2H participants, age might affect the motivation for language learning, as participants do not seem to fit into any of these four aspects of acculturation.

This situation of non-integration was observed for British retirees by both Ahmed (2011) and Rodriguez et al. (1998), who point out that in most cases, British retirees are not motivated to develop close contacts with the local population for various linguistic or ethno-physiological reasons like the Japanese in this study. We refer to this phenomenon as *contemplation*, whereby participants do not seek to be either integrated or assimilated to the host culture, or to be separated from their home culture. The MM2H programme is a unique case of immigration. Without distinct motivations to adapt to a local culture, participants have positioned themselves as observers who have come to enjoy their retired life as sojourners, not permanent residents. *Contemplation* can be connected to the relational ethics between participants and the local people in terms of understanding the basis of Aristotle's 'golden rule' that 'one should treat others as one would like others to treat oneself'. This concept of contemplation is based on the observation of the emotional adaptation of the Japanese retirees to the new environment since their needs are taken care of by Japanese agents or at least by individuals who have located for them a 'little Japan' in Malaysia. We submit that the ethics of *contemplation* is the process of entering into a new culture through an observation of its norms, values and behavioural patterns without losing the spirit of one's own culture. Furthermore, the retirees' reluctance to learn another language could also be related to maintaining their own ethnic identity since 'Which language people speak and the act of changing language ... can be important in how people see themselves' (Temple, 2008, p. 5). The participants in this study largely demonstrate 'a classic scenario' (Smallwood, 2007, p. 129) of lifestyle in the host country, that is, they find that when they arrive they can live according to their previous lifestyles without actually mixing with their hosts. The retirees in this study, for the reasons discussed, did not integrate into Malaysian society, and lived on its margins. Their retired status compounded their isolation, and reinforced the mono-cultural nature of their social networks.

The term 'social capital' (Putnam, 2000) can also be used to understand the connections between individuals. There are three types of social capital: bonding, which involves ties between people in similar situations; bridging, which involves making links outside of the immediate group and linking, which relates to much more distant ties. Retirees in this study used bonding as social capital primarily since they were limited by their language skills in English and the local languages. In such diasporic circumstances, it was pragmatic for them to seek out and create their own social networks. However, with their language limitations, these retirees failed to create social networks with the locals, which impinges on both the ethics and equity of their interactions with them.

Conclusion

The cultural behaviour of MM2H participants draws our attention to the ethical component of values by moving them from a consideration of objects to acts while virtue ethics moves beyond acts by creating the dilemma for the participants of making a choice or following the rules from being passive to active in terms of interaction. In the area of interpersonal interaction, equity is expressed through the demand for similar rights in the social system.

However, the interesting question is: Why do Japanese retirees, being in the minority, have no interest in a more profound relationship with the locals or demonstrate at least some interest in learning the local language? This question can be answered by referring to Lambek (2008) and Phillipson (2003). Lambek (2008, p. 134) says 'virtue ethics asks neither how we can acquire objects of value nor how we can do what is absolutely right, but how we should live and what kind of person we want to be'. It is interesting to note that in this modern age, there is discrepancy between the concepts of ethical value and economic value. As observed by Lambek (2008), ethical value is more subjectivized, whereas economic value in the eyes of society is fully objectivized. Phillipson (2003) connects the essence of language choice to the plane of relationship between economics and language, by noticing similarities between them. An 'analysis of the economics of language can clarify relationships between resources, allocations, and certain types of justice and efficiency, while reminding us that approaches in economics are not independent of value judgments' (Phillipson, 2003, p. 145). He points out that an economically strong society, dominant in certain places, may have an impact. 'Less powerful languages can become victims of linguicide as much from economic forces, the "laws" of the market, as state policies' (p. 145). We can assume that such considerations affect the choice of the participants of this study. They may not want to learn the local languages because of the perceived higher 'economic' status of English in Malaysia, where it is used and valued for economic purposes. Hence, being able to communicate in English is deemed sufficient for their economic needs.

It can be concluded that economic value is the link between the ethical values and behaviour of the participants of the study. Firstly, the main choice of the language of communication for both formal and informal situations is a subjective one. On the one hand, this choice facilitates the life of the immigrants, but on the other hand, it is a barrier in terms of developing intercultural relationships with the locals. Their choice of language indicates that the Japanese are much less concerned with cognitive matching (see Triandis, 1994) than Europeans are. The Japanese participants enjoy greater freedom in choosing the language of interaction with the locals as they can choose the language of communication they want from the options available to them. English is preferred because MM2H participants reside in places where there are other foreigners and locals who use English in their daily interactions. Moreover, English is also widely used in the major cities of Malaysia such as Kuala Lumpur and Penang and there is no real need to use the local languages although some participants who had studied Malay acknowledged that it is important to master the language since it is the national language of Malaysia. Obviously as stated by Oberg (1960, p. 145), '... language is the principal symbol of communication' and to ensure more meaningful communication then there is a need to show the interest in at least one local language.

The perception of the dominant position of English among participants derives from the fact that English is widely used in Malaysia, a multi-ethnic and multilingual country. Through English, participants can manage to enter the surface level of the local culture that is considered sufficient for them to live quite comfortably. Such a system of values for these participants can be summarized as a system where the major requirement can be identified as a culturally oriented urban concept of living. Here the predominance of a pleasure-seeking lifestyle is focused on the landscape or pleasantness of the climate with age-specific requirements as the central features for their choice. This may lead us to the understanding that equity in terms of the intercultural relationships between Japanese retirees and the locals, most probably depends on how both sides benefit from such relations. In other words, the equity of the relationship is mostly based on economic values where the host is more interested in economic gains while the Japanese are more interested in a pleasure-seeking lifestyle. While Japanese participation in the programme can be assumed to be mostly the product of international mass tourism, they can be regarded as long-term-stay tourists too.

On the other hand, as noted by Taylor (1994), any social community's basic human demands need to be recognized by the authorities in order to preserve their cultural and ethical values. To do this, he offers an extraordinary way which we refer to as the politics of 'equal dignity', where because the neutrality of liberal thoughts cannot accommodate all people of different cultural backgrounds, it is replaced with 'the politics of recognition' and the survival of minority cultures.

If we look at this concept from the small social environment of these Japanese retirees, we can see some signs of such a policy emanating from the Malaysian government as it has provided services such as 'Japan-like' individual medical services in the town where they reside complete with Japanese-speaking local staff members. This mutual interest between the authorities and the participants may lie upon an understanding of the concept of equity as explained earlier, but more for ensuring Japanese satisfaction with the programme.

Significantly, retirement migration is different from migration among people of working age in two ways. First, as retirees are no longer working, their opportunities for participation in the host country are limited too. Furthermore, as noted previously, these retirees used the social capital of bonding (Putnam, 2000), which has compounded their situation of isolation from the wider local society. They were unable to 'bridge' with people outside of their ethnic group, because they did not speak the local languages. They were unable to assimilate with their hosts because they lived on the margins of Malaysian society, maintaining their boundaries of exclusion.

From the evidence, we can conclude that learning local languages and integrating into Malaysian society are not the aims of the retirees participating in the programme, although learning local languages can provide them with certain advantages in developing deeper levels of communication with the local communities in Malaysia. At the same time, Malaysians should be made aware of the MM2H programme in order to be hospitable towards the participants, thus ensuring that social equity can be achieved for both parties. In any case, the MM2H programme was not designed towards providing cross-cultural opportunities. It focused on the economic benefits. Nevertheless, by participating in this programme, the retirees, the guests, are able to enjoy a desirable lifestyle of their choice which we have termed *contemplation* while the government, the host, profits economically from it.

This study has implications for equity in the need to learn the local languages. Being able to communicate in English alone is not sufficient for intercultural relationships to develop with the local community as discussed earlier. Additionally, higher levels of language competence are required in both English and the local languages for more meaningful interpersonal communication to take place. Another way to increase social equity is to encourage the exchange of knowledge of cultural traditions. Programmes to facilitate this should be organized by the agencies involved in the programme as part of their responsibilities in easing the retirees into the host country. It is recommended that future studies focus on the nature of the socio-cultural aspects of the programme with particular regard to the nature of the social and communication costs involved in living away from the homeland.

Acknowledgements

This work was supported by the grant for Japan-related research projects provided by the Sumitomo Foundation 2008 (088411).

References

Ahmed, A. (2011). Belonging out of context: The intersection of place, networks and ethnic identity among retired British migrants in the Costa Blanca. *Journal of Identity and Migration Studies, 5*(2), 2–19.

AON. (2010). *European workers want to retire abroad…and ideally to the sun.* Retrieved December 7, 2010, from http://aon.mediaroom.com/index.php?s=43&item=1987

Berry, J.W. (1997). Immigration, acculturation and adaptation. *Applied Psychology: An International Review, 46*, 5–34.

Bradley, D., & Bradley, M. (Eds.). (2002). *Language endangerment and language maintenance.* London: Routledge Curzon.

Chibocos, T.R., Leite, R.W., & Weis, D.L. (2005). *Readings in family theory.* Thousand Oaks, CA: Sage.

Crystal, D. (2003). *English as a global language* (2nd ed.). Cambridge: Cambridge University Press.

Degefa, A. (2004, January 12–16). *Criteria for language choice in multilingual societies: An appraisal of Ethiopian language choice at the Federal level.* IACL, Santiago de Chile.

Dumanig, F. (2007, July 26–28). *Analysis on the language choice and marital typology of South-East Asian couples.* 2nd Singapore Graduate Forum on Southeast Asia Studies.

Fasold, R. (1990). *The sociolinguistics of language.* Oxford: Blackwell.

Ferrer, R., & Sankoff, D. (2004). Transmission, education and integration in projections of language shift in Valencia. *Language Policy, 3*, 107–131.

Foo, B., & Richards, C. (2004). English in Malaysia. *RELC Journal, 35*, 229–240.

Gal, S. (1979). *Language shift: Social determinants of linguistic change in bilingual Australia.* New York: Academic Press.

Ip, D., Wu, C.T., & Inglis, C. (1998). Settlement experiences of Taiwanese immigrants in Australia. *Asian Studies Review, 22*, 79–97.

Johansson, S. (1991). *Language use in mixed marriage.* Retrieved June 17, 2005, from http://hem.hj.se/~lsj/bl/bl.pdf

Kaur, K. (1995). Why they need English in Malaysia: A survey. *World Englishes, 14*, 223–230.

Kawahara, M. (2010). Adaptive strategy of Japanese senior long-term stayers and local community responses in Chiangmai. *The Journal of Thai Studies, 10*, 35–55.

King, R., Warnes, T., & Williams, A. (2000). *Sunset lives?: British retirement migration to the Mediterranean.* Oxford: Berg.

Koike, I. (1993). A comparative view of English – Teaching policies in an international world with a focus on Japanese TEFL policy. In *Georgetown University Roundtable on Languages and Linguistics* (pp. 275–284). Washington, DC: Georgetown University Press.

Kubo, T., & Ishikawa, Y. (2004). Searching for 'paradise': Japanese international retirement migration. *Japanese Journal of Human Geography, 56*(3), 74–87.

Lambek, M. (2008). Value and virtue. *Anthropological Theory, 8*, 133–157.

Li Wei. (1994). *Three generations, two languages, one family. Language choice and language shift in a Chinese community in Britain.* Clevedon: Multilingual Matters.

Lim Hua Sing. (1984). Japanese perspectives on Malaysia's 'Look East' policy. *Journal of Southeast Asian Affairs*, 231–245.

Malaysia My Second Home Programme. Retrieved June 17, 2012, from http://www.mm2h.gov.my

Nagatomo, J. (2007). The social transformation of the Japanese society in the 1990s and the Japanese migration to Australia: The relationship between the changes in lifestyle values and migration decision. *The Otemon Journal of Australian Studies, 33*, 177–200.

Nair-Venugopal, S. (2001). The sociolinguistics of choice in Malaysian business settings. *International Journal of the Sociology of Language, 152*, 21–52.

Nair-Venugopal, S. (2003). Intelligibility in English: Of what relevance today to intercultural communication? *Language and Intercultural Communication, 3*(1), 36–47.

Oberg, K. (1960). Culture shock: Adjustment to new cultural environments. *Practical Anthropology, 7*, 177–182. Reprinted as Migration, Medizinethnologie zu Hause und Islamishe Kultur in Europa heute. *Curare, 29*(2+3), 142–146 (2006).

Ono, M. (2008). Long-stay tourism and international retirement migration: Japanese retires in Malaysia. *Transnational Migration in East Asia Senri Ethnological Reports, 77*, 151–162.

Phillipson, R. (2003). *English-only Europe?: Challenging language policy.* London: Routledge.

Powell, R., & Hashim, A. (2011). Language disadvantage in Malaysian litigation and arbitration. *World Englishes, 30*(1), 92–105.

Putnam, R.D. (2000). *Bowling alone. The collapse and revival of American community.* New York: Simon and Schuster.

Rodriguez, V., Fernandez-Mayoralas, G., & Rojo, F. (1998). European retirees on the Costa del Sol: A cross-national comparison. *International Journal of Population Geography, 4*, 183–200.

Sato, M. (2001). *Farewell to Nippon: Lifestyle migrants in Australia.* Melbourne: Trans Pacific Press.

Smallwood, D. (2007). The integration of British migrants in Aquitaine. In C. Geoffroy & R. Sibley (Eds.), *Going abroad. Travel, tourism and migration: Cross cultural perspectives on mobility* (pp. 119–131). Cambridge: Cambridge Scholars Publishing.

Spolsky, B. (2004). *Language policy: Key topics in sociolinguistics.* Cambridge: Cambridge University Press.

Stapa, S.H., Amzah, N., Hieda, N., & Musaev, T. (2010). Investigating social issues among the Japanese adapting Malaysia as a second home. *Proceedings of the Fourth International Malaysia–Thailand Conference on Southeast Asian Studies*, Fakulti Sains Sosial dan Kemanusiaan, Universiti Kebangsaan Malaysia.

The Star. (2012, June 15). More Japanese opt to live in Malaysia.

Stephanenko, T. (2004). *Ethnopsychology.* Moscow: Aspekt Press.

Taylor, C. (1994). *Multiculturalism: Examining the politics of recognition.* Princeton, NJ: Princeton University Press.

Temple, B. (2008). Investigating language and identity in cross-language narratives. *Migrations and Identities, 1*(1), 1–18.

Thibaut, J.W., & Kelly, H.H. (1959). *The social psychology of groups.* New York: Wiley.

Triandis, H. (1994). *Culture and social behavior.* New York: McGraw-Hill.

Walster, E., Walster, G.W., & Bersheid, E. (1978). *Equity: Theory and research.* Boston: Allyn & Bacon.

Warnes, A., King, R., Williams, A., & Patterson, G. (1999). The well-being of British expatriate retirees in southern Europe. *Ageing and Society, 19*, 717–740.

World Bank. Retrieved September 6, 2011, from http://web.worldbank.org/

Yau, F.M. (1997). Code switching and language choice in the Hong Kong legislative council. *Journal of Multilingual and Multicultural Development, 18*(1), 40–52.

The in-depth interview as a research tool for investigating the online intercultural communication of Asian Internet users in relation to ethics in intercultural research

Doris Fetscher

Department of Applied Languages and Intercultural Communication, Westsächsische Hochschule Zwickau, Dr.-Friedrichs-Ring 2A, Zwickau, Germany

Virtual intercultural communication is of great interest in intercultural research. How can a researcher gain access to this field of investigation if s/he does not or only partially speaks the languages used by the subjects? This study is an example of how categories relevant to research can be accessed through in-depth interviews. The interview method generates an interactive awareness process to which both partners contribute in equal measure, and which complies with the requirements of intercultural research ethics.

Für die interkulturelle Forschung ist die virtuelle interkulturelle Kommunikation von großem Interesse. Wie kann ein Forscher Zugang zu diesem Untersuchungsfeld gewinnen, wenn er die dort verwendeten Sprachen nicht oder nur teilweise spricht. Die Untersuchung zeigt exemplarisch wie mit der Methode des problemzentrierten Interviews ein Zugang zu forschungsrelevanten Kategorien gefunden werden kann. Die Interviewmethode generiert einen interaktiven Erkenntnisprozess, zu dem beide Interviewpartner gleichberechtigt beitragen und der den Anforderungen an eine interkulturelle Forschungsethik gerecht wird.

Introduction

Virtual space has radically changed in the last 10 years. Virtual social networks like Facebook and Twitter have spread in a totally unpredictable way. Access to the Internet via Smartphones has opened the virtual space to a wider range of people all over the world and connects more and more people from different language and cultural backgrounds. The everyday life of many people has been extended, especially in the last few years, to an equally everyday virtual environment.

A large number of research projects have dealt with this phenomenon, taking into consideration linguistic and intercultural aspects as well. For instance, the title of Naomi S. Baron's volume is *Always On. Language in an Online and Mobile World* (2008). Many of the linguistically oriented studies on language on the Internet early on expressed the hope that the spread of the Internet would lead to more diversity, more exchange and understanding worldwide, and consequently to more equity in a political sense. David Crystal (2006) quotes: 'Tyler Chambers, creator of various web language projects, agrees: "the future of the Internet is even more multilingual and cross-cultural exploration and understanding than we've already seen'" (p. 235). The fact that more and more people all over the world have been able to gain access to the Internet was considered optimistically and in an idealized manner as a contribution to democratization.

For the Thai philosopher Saraj Hongladarom (n.d.), 'it is this higher frequency of interpenetration which will influence intercultural communication in a "natural" way.' He describes the process as follows:

> My point is only that, whatever these shared values and ideals turn out to be, the Internet is instrumental in bringing them about, for whatever exactly these values are, they are the necessary presuppositions on which communication among cultures is possible. As the Internet is facilitating more of such communication, at least a way is there for these presuppositions, this set of shared values and ideals, to develop themselves. The Internet will also facilitate interpenetrations, each culture giving something to others and receiving something in return.

The editors of the newly published volume *New Media and Intercultural Communication*, Pauline Hope Cheong, Judith N. Martin, and Leah P. Macfadyen (2012), likewise engage in this discourse and position themselves in a very nuanced and critical manner. While they do see the positive potential of computer-mediated communication (CMC) in promoting greater equity with regard to gender or democratic processes such as the role of new media in the democratization efforts in the Middle East, they nevertheless point to the danger of 'elimination of Otherness' through our willingness 'to reduce both ourselves and others on social networking sites to standardized commodities [. . .]' (p. xvii). The authors counter this argument with a clearly formulated ethical aspiration.

> An important aspect of this book is that it brings to the foreground for us one of the primary *ethical* impulses that underlies much of our interest in both the potentially salutary as well as the potentially destructive impacts of CMC; namely, a foundational sense of responsibility for 'the Other.' (p. xvii)

To regard the user separately from his/her cultural background, to disregard his/her multiple, complex, and culturally variable beliefs, practices, norms, and sense of identity, is considered by the authors as a 'form of violence against the Other' (p. xvii). They, however, do not initiate a discussion about methodology in the Foreword. Taking into consideration this aspiration, my paper deals with two questions that are hierarchically related. The first overall methodological question is this: Is the in-depth interview suited to gain insights into the virtual multilingual environments and communicative practices of German-speaking colleagues of Asian descent? The second subordinated question that in-depth interviews target is: Which intercultural problems and cultural differences are relevant to the interview partners themselves, and how do they make them relevant?

Research on virtual intercultural communication, especially on intercultural virtual teamwork, shows that the classical intercultural misunderstandings and difficulties, which were already known from face-to-face contact, were reproduced in virtual collaboration in spite of the use of common sites and technology (Fetscher, 2010). Justine Cassell and Dona Tversky (2005) give a good overview of the previous literature. However, the situation in the current widespread social networks is different. Generally, social networks such as Facebook do not specifically promote collaboration. They promote the exchange of information, self-manifestation, networking, and cross-linking in the hypertext (see, for instance, the chapter on Facebook in Baron, 2008). A recent overview of studies of intercultural problems in CMC can be found in Beth Bonniwell Haslett (2012).

The focus of my investigation is therefore an indirect examination of CMC. There are two reasons for this: First of all, I only partially speak the languages with which the interviewees communicate online, and I do not have any experience living in the Asian cultural context. Aside from that, I as a researcher can approach a culture that is foreign to me only with my biographically constructed prior understanding that is colored by my culture, as stated by Norbert Schröer (2009, pp. 102–109).

The qualitative interview can balance these shortcomings, if we assume that it enables the establishment of a common practice within a virtually shared situation (Kvale & Brinkmann, 2009). This generates a reciprocal insight by negotiating different meanings. Such a mutual and consciously initiated cognitive process is the basis of all intercultural competence and thus, it should be considered as central in all intercultural research. I think that the respect of and responsibility toward the Other is methodologically very well realized in this reciprocity. In addition, I hope to find, following Hongladarom, an answer to the question of what effect the higher frequency of intercultural communication on the Internet has on my interview partners from their point of view, and how they present the way they deal with difference and diversity.

German universities of applied sciences aspire to clearly link teaching and research with respect to their application to the students' future professional life. For this reason, my work is also pedagogically and didactically motivated. We urgently need to develop practicable research settings for the methodological training of students in the course Intercultural Communication. With the help of such research settings, the students can then continue to work on their intercultural competence on their own. CMC, with which they are inevitably confronted in their professional and private lives, is a very important area in this regard. In her article 'Dialogic Ethics, Cosmopolitanism, and Intercultural Communication,' Kathleen Glenister Roberts (2008) writes:

> First communication scholars educate communication students who enter and deeply impact the marketplace. We ignore that fact at our own peril. Second and more importantly, economics and the marketplace do matter to cosmopolitism. [...] it is worth noting that a theory of cosmopolitanism is impossible without attention to the everyday practices – discursive and otherwise – of diverse groups. (pp. 89–90)

Multiple methods in CMC research

The methods used to investigate CMC are varied. Frequently, one encounters a mix of quantitative and qualitative approaches. Online surveys on the one hand and in-depth interviews on the other hand play an important role in this regard. *Research Methods in Human–Computer Interaction* by Jonathan Lazar, Jinjuan Heidi Feng, and Harry Hochheiser (2010), for example, gives a useful overview of methodological approaches, although technical issues and not sociological or linguistic questions are the focus. Sirpa Leppänen, Anne Pitkänen-Huhta, Arja Piirainen-Marsh, Tarja Nikula, and Saija Peuronen (2009) illustrate how different qualitative approaches as visual tasks (e.g. photographs and collages) and literacy diaries can be combined:

'This was done with the help of multiple methods including several group and individual discussions with the participants' (p. 1084). Conducting qualitative studies requires a high level of proficiency and intercultural competence of the researcher. Jan Kruse, Stephanie Bethmann, Debora Niermann, and Christian Schmieder (2012) recently published the edited volume *Qualitative Interviewforschung in und mit fremden Sprachen*. This is the first time that a comprehensive collection of articles on the issue was published in the German language. Aglaja Przyborski and Monika Wohlrab-Sahr (2008) postulate in general for the participation of native speakers in research teams, where the empirical data are culturally and linguistically very distant from the cultural and linguistic background of the researchers even if the researchers speak the given languages:

> [. . .] Precisely when it comes to interpreting the manner of representation and not simply the mere content of what has been said, one should be careful with judging one's own linguistic competence. Slang, the tone of voice, an allusion or ironic shading can easily escape a non-native speaker. In this case, life experiences with and in the relevant field are often more important than formal linguistic competence. (p. 308; translation mine)

In many publications about CMC, the issue of the researcher's language or intercultural competence is not explicitly addressed. Many studies, far more in the literature published in the English-speaking than in the German-speaking world, are ideally conducted by a native speaker researcher or a multicultural research team. Native speaker subjects, especially international students, are recruited for surveys on their second language, the language of the researcher, as in Robert Shuter (2012): 'First, college-educated Indian women were contacted with the assistance of Campus International at a Midwestern university' (p. 212). Since Shuter was interested in data pertaining to the text-messaging behavior of Indian women in India, he emphasizes in his article that the 16 subjects all spent less than two years in the USA, meaning that they were still close enough to their Indian cultural roots to be able to make relevant statements. Methodological statements about possible intercultural issues of conducting an interview, such as summarized, for instance, by Bettina Beer (2007) or Björn Alpermann (2012), are rarely explicitly addressed and made relevant for the research process.

The questions are different for virtual environments such as Facebook pages or blogs. In these cases, one is dealing with multilingual data written by people from different cultural backgrounds, not always only in their native language, but also in foreign or second languages or in mixed languages. Playing with the diversity of languages is widespread and productive in CMC. The largest number of different varieties and forms of 'multi-voicedness' and heteroglossy could be observed among young people. The more complex the users interconnect/interlink, the more translocal or hybrid the communication and play with languages and identities, the more difficult researching these data becomes (see Fetscher, 2009; Leppänen et al., 2009).

The in-depth interview in intercultural research

In German, the interview form that was chosen for this study is called 'problemzen-triert.' In the English translation, one finds the terms 'focused' or 'in-depth.' For the study at hand, this interview form was chosen because it takes place as a co-present interaction (face-to-face or by telephone) where both, the interviewer and the interviewee, participate in the process of understanding. For Andreas Witzel (2000) the main characteristic of a 'problem centered' interview consists of establishing a process of understanding for both participants. He considers this process as an interplay between induction and deduction. Subjective narrations of issues are initiated in an in-depth interview by guided and theory-driven questions. These narrations can then be complemented by dialogues in which the interview partners try to establish common ground and mutual understanding. This interactional aspect of in-depth interviews is particularly valuable for intercultural research since an ethnocentric approach can be avoided and the interview partners can have equal participation in the generation of knowledge. The categories that arise inductively can then be processed into a working hypothesis and examined deductively in further studies. The interactional approach also prevents an essentialist attribution of cultural categories by the researcher.

Questions in an in-depth interview are first posed in as general and open a manner as possible. Lazar et al. (2010) present the advantages of such a procedure in the following:

> By asking questions that explore a wide range of concerns about a problem and giving interviewees the freedom to provide detailed responses, researchers can use interviews to gather data that would otherwise be very hard to capture. Given a chance to talk, and questions that encourage reflection and consideration, interviewees may go on at great length, generating ideas and sharing insides that would have been lost to surveys. (p. 178)

To better compare the interviews, the following guide with seven very general and open questions and a summarizing last question was developed.

(1) What do you think of first in connection with the topic Intercultural Communication on the Internet?
(2) Which medium do you use for this purpose?
(3) In which languages do you write?
(4) Are you able to notice differences in communication with speakers of other cultural backgrounds? Do you think these differences are due to the differences in cultural background? (Examples)
(5) Has your writing or communicative style changed with virtual communication? (In German, in English, in your native language)
(6) Does the daily use of new media affect the writing process for instance of emails, posts/comments.
(7) Have relationships changed through virtual communication, and if so, how? (Social networks, quality of relationship)
(8) What should I watch out for when I communicate virtually with Taiwanese/Koreans/Filipinos?

The interviewees

The three interview partners come from Taiwan, Korea, and the Philippines. All of the interviewees are multilingual. They lived for several years in Germany or still live there. They all did studies in intercultural communication. Two of them communicate daily on Facebook and other virtual social networks. The interviews were conducted in German. They are focused, guided, and open.

The interview partners were selected because they were equipped with theoretical knowledge about intercultural communication and because they were familiar with the interviewer as their relationship can be described as friendly and cooperative. Although the interview situation was asymmetrical, a close relationship can strongly support the quality of dialogicity and reflexivity as is desirable in an in-depth interview. The following first excerpt from the interview with L. shows a dialogue sequence in which common ground is established through the interviewer's lack of background knowledge about the language situation in Manila and the interviewee's personal biography. Because the interviews were conducted in German, the following examples have been translated into English by the author. The German transcriptions were based on the conventions of GAT 2. These conventions could not be considered in the translation. As my analysis is primarily content-oriented, this method is justifiable.

The interviewees – L., Filipina, 53 – establishing common ground

At the beginning of the face-to-face interview, L., Filipina, 53 years old, declares: 'Facebook has changed my life a lot.' L. grew up in a multilingual and multicultural diplomatic environment. As a child, she lived seven years in Mexico and six years in Germany. She speaks Spanish and German without an accent. In 1974, she returned to Manila and stayed there until 2005, when she came back to Germany. She still lives in Germany, working as a research assistant. The languages she uses on the Internet are: English, Taglish, Tagalog, German, and Spanish. The media she actively uses are: email (two accounts, private and professional), Skype, Yahoo Messenger, and Facebook (about 200 friends). She makes more passive use of a Filipino diaspora network and different linguistic networks.

During the interview there is a dialogue sequence, as early as minute 11–16, in which the interviewer had to ask several times about the use of Taglish and Tagalog in order to correctly understand the interviewee's statements. It is interesting in this regard that the interviewee initially states that she communicates in Tagalog and then corrects herself once and then at another time after the interviewer seeks clarification and states that she actually does not communicate in Tagalog but in Taglish, the non-standard code-switching variety:

00:12:00
Interviewer: So you actually write in all languages?
L.: I actually write in four in four languages. German, English, Tagalog and Spanish, or rather not really pure Tagalog but the code-switching variety actually.

And a bit later:

00:13:02
L.: And to my friends in the Philippines I write to them mainly in English, but I tone it down with with Tagalog or with the code-switching variety. But that is really normal in our country.
Interviewer: Mhm. That means they are would you then say the things are trilingual? Tagalog, English and Tag Taglish?
L.: I would say it is English and Taglish as well. So I would say only two get mixed.

Interviewer: Only two? Yes?
L.: Yes, mainly two. I cannot speak pure Tagalog. That is impossible. So I always mix English and Tagalog.

The interviewer's statements mirror the competitive relationship that exists between Tagalog and Taglish as official national language on the one hand and spoken language on the other hand. In addition, insecurity is revealed when attempting to differentiate between the code-switching variety Taglish and Tagalog.

Later the interviewer asks for an explanation of this matter and gains an insight into the interviewee's personal language biography.

00:14:15
Interviewer: Now you just said Tagalog is not possible. Why?
L.: Because I don't. Tagalog may be my native language so to speak but I grew up speaking Spanish and I would say Spanish is the first language that I consciously learned. And uh our mother did not speak to us in Tagalog at home but in Spanish. And then came Germany. And it was only at sixteen that I learned my own language. There was really no book. There was really no method. So I just picked it up. So like a kind of natural acquisition not an instructed acquisition. And that is why I am not sure now if that is correct although I spent 30 years in my country. I never learned it the proper way. I mean people do not speak pure Tagalog most people, if they are not Tagalog. It is the national language, but not the native language of everyone [...] That is why I only speak English and this Taglish this mixture this code-switching.

Because the interviewer had a hard time understanding the language situation in Manila, the interviewee sent her some Facebook examples in Taglish on the day of the interview (see Figure 1).

Roger M. Thompson (2003) gives a very good introduction to language use in the Philippines including a historical perspective. In 1973, President Ferdinand Marcos declared '[...] that English and Pilipino were the official languages and that Filipino should be developed as a common national language' (p. 37). However, for the most part, educated Filipinos rejected Tagalog neologisms.

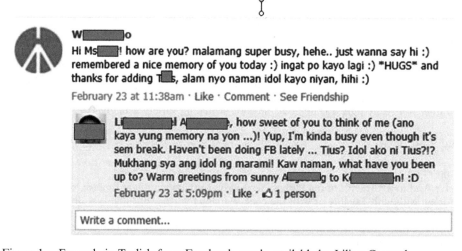

Figure 1. Example in Taglish from Facebook, made available by Lilian Coronel.

They simply mixed the familiar English word into their Tagalog academic discourse. Their mixing of English and Tagalog, at first called halo-halo 'mix-mix,' Engalog, and then Taglish, spread rapidly from the classroom to the general populace through radio and television [...] Today nearly all educated Filipinos, including those in high places, use Taglish except in formal situations when only 'pure' English or 'pure' Tagalog may be used. (p. 41)

All over the world we can find similar situations, in post-colonial contexts, where former dominant languages are substituted by mixed languages which are usually used as spoken languages. Thompson also declares that 'Taglish has become an auxiliary spoken language with no body of literature except in tabloids' (2003, p. 41). Thompson does not consider the use of Taglish as a written language on the Internet in his study. Rather he focuses on television, radio, and movies. Whether the fact of writing Taglish on the Internet will induce processes of standardization is another very promising field of linguistic research. We still don't know whether Internet communication should be considered more as a literal discourse or as an oral discourse. Most research in this field opted for a solution in between, referring to 'conceptual orality.' The acceptance of non-standard language use in social networks, the greater tolerance for mistakes, for example, in English or German used as a lingua franca or as a second language may lead to a de-hegemonization of the standard varieties. On the other hand, non-standard varieties may be affected by processes of standardization. The shift in both directions can be considered as a movement to more equity in the use of written language, where standards are devalued on the one hand and non-standard varieties are upgraded on the other hand.

The interviewees – F., Taiwanese, 30

At the beginning of the telephone interview F. uses nearly the same words as L. to explain her relationship with Facebook: 'Facebook has changed my life.' F. is about 30 years old and currently lives with her German husband in Taiwan, where she is working as a teacher for Chinese as a foreign language. F. studied in Germany and the UK for seven years. She finished her studies in Germany and lived there for two years with her German husband. She communicates regularly on the Internet in Mandarin, English, German, and Japanese. She actively uses the following media: email, MSN Messenger, Skype, Facebook (about 80 friends), and visits the blogs of friends more passively but also regularly.

Contrary to L. who declares using only one language for one posting, F. states that language change within one posting is very common in the communication with her friends. She often switches from Mandarin to German or English with friends from Taiwan and China who use German or English as a second language.

The interviewees – M., Korean, 30

For M., 'Facebook is not so important!' M. has been living in Austria with her German husband and her two children since 2010. She began her studies in Germany in 1998. Actually, she stays at home with her children. M. communicates in Korean, German, and English. She actively uses email and Skype and regularly visits Korean web pages and blogs of friends. The interview also took place on the telephone.

Filipino 'chain-posting' – culture-specific genres

The second example I want to show is also extracted from the interview with L. and has been selected because it illustrates very well the process of becoming aware of differences, which can also be generated through the in-depth interview. This process is characterized by the difficulty of ascribing these differences to culture. L. is not sure if the differences she has discovered are not more related to personality or the medium Facebook than to culture.

Schröer (2009) refers to the dialogicity of each understanding as the basic insight of hermeneutic epistemology when he describes the ethnographer's special dilemma:

> The ethnographer is in a special way without orientation when he works out the culture-specific framework of interpretation, and he only has highly limited possibilities at his disposal to independently relate inevitably fragmentary and reactive research situations to a general framework and thus in a way to control them. (p. 104; translation mine)

In terms of method, it is therefore a greater advantage for the interviewee to ask that a culture-specific framework of interpretation be worked out.

Interviewer: Do you notice differences depending on culture?

00:18:32
L.: There is, I think, if it would be possible to discover something related to culture, then I would say so, but I am not sure if it is possible to generalize it in this way, it is that Filipinos have the strong tendency to send me funny things and to share them with me, much more than the Germans. But I don't know if this is not related more to personality than to culture. Because I also know Filipinos, but they have spent a lot of time in the USA, who have the tendency to send me more serious things. For example, what they have learnt in Meditation or Tai Chi . . .

00:20:28
L.: Not in the emails, but much more on Skype and Facebook, I think, cultural things are more obvious.
Interviewer: Could you give me an example for the funny things the Filipinos send, when you tell me that they forward much more funny things.

00:20:28
L.: Yes, that's in the emails. In Facebook, I don't know whether you have noticed it, that they tell you for example: if you know somebody who has had cancer, you should post the following message at least for one week on your wall. Or, it will soon be mother's day, then the people change their profile pictures and put a photo of their mother or themselves with their mother. And in most cases these were Filipinos. I didn't notice this in the posts of Germans or other nationalities.

00:22:02
L.: Yes, this is very striking; what else could it be? That one does only copy what the other has posted, and makes a proper post of it. I think that it is Filipinos who do this. You have to ask Elsa whether they do this, but I didn't notice that with Germans. But I don't know if this is related to culture. But I think that this is also related to the medium Facebook.

Two examples were also made available to me by L. (see Figure 2).

It is obvious that people's walls on Facebook generate new virtual genres. I could not find a clear label for the example in Figure 2. The phenomenon cannot really be considered as chain-posting, which is defined by WikiFAQs as follows:

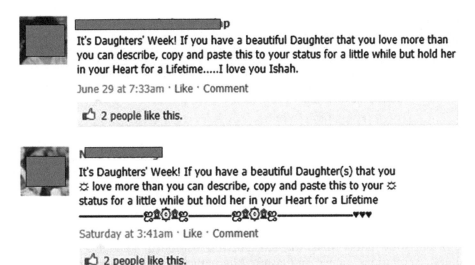

Figure 2. Example of Filipino "chain-posting" from Facebook, made available by Lilian Coronel.

> Chain Posting is the act of quoting the message of another user without adding anything to the discussion, which is then quoted by another user until the quoted messages become nothing more than a list of usernames and post times with the original message. Because of their lengthy nature and general lack of purpose, chain posting is considered a fad. (http://wikifaqs.net/index.php?title=Chain_Posting)

In our case the posting is personalized by another photograph and some textual alterations. In the second example, a graphical line has been added. From a German point of view (if we postulate previously internalized cultural categories) the text and also the graphics would probably be judged as kitsch (see Gevorgyan & Manucharova, 2009, for different web design preferences). A Daughters' week does not exist in Germany, so the institutional cause for these postings is culturally determined and I could not find a German version of this posting. However, I finally came up with a comparable German version for a Filipino posting of the same type (see Figure 3).

German posting

> I was born in the 1980s, grew up in the 1990s. We are the last generation that played on the street, the first that played video games and the last that recorded songs from the radio on cassette, we are the pioneers of the Walkman era. We learned how to use the video recorder, played Atari, Super Nintendo and Game Boy. We are the generation of Thunder Cats, Power Rangers, Ninja Turtles, Transformers. We lived without a mobile phone, three of us rode on a bicycle for many kilometres because our mother didn't drive for us. We did not have 99 channels, flat screen TVs, surround sound, MP3, iPod, Facebook or Twitter ... And yet we had a great time! Post this as your status if you too are a happy child of the 80s ♥ (29 November 14:37). (translation mine)

The two postings seem to treat the same subject: the nostalgia of a childhood without the Internet and all other types of technical gadgets. In the German text, the list of gadgets is longer, while the Filipino posting expresses the gratitude to the parents for a good childhood. This aspect is totally missing in the German posting.

R

When I was a kid, I didn't have a laptop, iPod, Blackberry, PS3, Wifi or designer dresses. I played outside with friends, bruised my knees, made up stories and played hide and seek... I ate what my mom made. I would think twice before I said "no" to my parents! Life wasn't hard, it was good & I survived.
Re-post this if you appreciate the way you were raised. Thanks to my parents, for making me who I am!

18 hours ago · Like · Comment

👍 9 people like this.

Figure 3.   Example of another Filipino "chain-posting" from Facebook, made available by Lilian Coronel.

It contains even an underlying critique of mothers who drive their children everywhere they want to go to by car. Which path did this posting take around the virtual world and in which way has it been transformed or adapted to the proper cultural expectations, values, and tastes? Alternatively, is the analogy only a product of chance, or even a normal phenomenon of globalization? Would a German share the Filipino posting without eliminating the passage of gratitude to the parents? I really don't think so.

The chain-postings can be considered virtual rituals, following the definition of Hubert Knoblauch and Helga Kotthoff (2001) (as cited in Kotthoff, 2009):

> [rituals] bind the group together, inspire joint action and structure the social reality. They have a beginning and an end and thus a time structure. By highlighting expressive and aesthetic dimensions they also stimulate emotional and metaphysical experiences of participants. (p. 173)

In this sense, L.'s wall offers the opportunity to share a specific ritual. Theoretically, such a ritual could spread, adapting to the cultural knowledge of the other cultural groups present on the wall. It is not certain that the interpenetration does really work in this way, but I think that these observations can be taken as a point of departure for further research on virtual rituals and their potential for construction of culture in the social networks. Joonsoeng Lee (2012), for example, makes an impressive connection between the development of virtual memorial zones and ritual changes in Korea in his paper 'Rite of Death as a Popular Commodity: Neoliberalism, Media, and New Korean Funeral Culture.'

It happens 'so quickly very quickly.' Interferences of routines in virtual communication in the native language

In the following example, F. from Taiwan remembers a critical incident with her boss in Taiwan, which took place via email (see Hennig, 2012, for the determination and definition of critical incidents and Fetscher, 2010, for virtual critical incidents). As is the case in other examples, the process of becoming aware can be observed here. In addition, the example illustrates very well what Will Baker (2011) defines as intercultural awareness in a multilingual environment:

> Intercultural awareness is the conscious understanding of the role that culturally based forms, practices and frames of reference can have in intercultural communication and

the ability to put these conceptions into practice in a flexible a context-specific manner in real time communication. (p. 202)

Baker's research is based on ELF (English as a lingua franca) communication and on real-time communication. In our case, F. is communicating in her native language via email but even so, she cannot avoid the interference of a different German politeness routine in written communication. This kind of interference, which can emerge even in native–native conversations when people are acting daily in two or more different cultural and linguistic registers, is still not sufficiently considered in intercultural research.

Nevertheless, none of the current characterizations of intercultural competence and cultural awareness have fully explored the relationships between cultures and language and the way intercultural competence may operate in intercultural communication in global lingua franca contexts. (p. 201)

The following example shows F.'s difficulties in choosing the correct register in Mandarin and in changing routines very quickly:

Interviewer: Do the culturally different styles of communication influence one another?

00:42:48
F.: One concrete example: [giggling] I think that just recently, before coming to Germany, I had a short email communication with my boss in Chinese and I really noticed that I really think that there was an interference of my style in Chinese, and my boss, she assumed that I was much too lax. That's true, But she adopted the style. That was really funny. She wrote me a very informal email. But as I know her she is not the type of person who writes in a casual style. Very funny. Exactly. Normally she always wrote in a very correct way, after all in teaching languages this is very important and for this she is used to a correct style. It's true, I really wrote a very informal Chinese email. Later I realized, oh dear, how could I write such an email to my boss, so-so. I am very happy that she didn't take it as an offense. I corrected my mistake very quickly.

00:44:06
F.: Yes, because my mother always tells me, ahh, I have to adjust my style. But, I tell you, that is really true, it is so difficult. It happens so quickly, very quickly. I cannot manage it so quickly. For example, I have to deal with Chinese people and I have to change immediately into the Chinese style and when there is a German in front of me, immediately into the German style. Sometimes I use the wrong style and often you put your foot in your mouth.

In the first part of the example, F. describes how she became aware that she had adopted the wrong register with her boss ('I was much too lax'). In her answer, the boss adopts the same informal style, which is very unusual for her. F. does not immediately recognize the indirect way in which the boss is expressing her criticism. It takes her some time to understand that this is not funny at all. This incident shows very well the interpenetration of social practices and their underlying values, and how they can be negotiated in email communication.

In the second part of the example, F. does not make an exact distinction between virtual and face-to-face communication ('when there is a German in front of me'). This happens often in the interview with F. and sometimes also in the other two interviews.

In general, L. and M. describe their strategies for controlling the different registers. L. even uses the expression 'argot' (secret language) to describe how she excludes and includes the different groups on her wall only through language choice. In this way, she tries to avoid the situation where certain postings, which are acceptable for one cultural group, could be face threatening for another group. L. explains that when her wall was getting more and more multicultural, she was afraid that her German friends could be shocked by her Filipino style of writing, which could be considered as 'kitsch.' L. and M. recognize that written communication offers many more possibilities of controlling, but at the same time the daily use of media brings about a routine characterized by very quick reactions not reflected upon.

As a non-sinologist, it would be impossible for me to study this problem with primary data. For the proper collection of critical incidents in intercultural research, they have to be validated by experts of the cultures involved, in order to guarantee that they really reflect standardized behavior (Heringer, 2004). In the case at hand, both interview partners have had intercultural training and do not doubt the attribution to culturally specific and linguistically pragmatic standards. [For further reading and investigation of critical incidents, that is, narratives of intercultural misunderstandings, see Hennig, 2012.] These incidents can be used, even without teaching guidelines, for intercultural sensitivity training of Germans who are preparing for virtual cooperation with Chinese. It would then be important to collect examples like how a transposition of the Chinese polite style into the German style could look like. In the German-speaking world, studies by Susanne Günthner (1993) on intercultural communication between Germans and Chinese using conversational analysis are notable.

'I am still very, very conservative' – *normative controlling and other types of resistance*

Culture change is always characterized by push-and-pull factors. In their classical study about migration, Andrea Hettlage-Varjas and Robert Hettlage (1984) describe the process of identification as follows:

> Each mature identification process consists of approaches and rejections, self-denials and self-confirmations... One changes points of view and slowly sheds those aspects which one has slowly outgrown. Thus, assuming new roles is possible. (p.380; translation mine)

If we want to know how a person is acting in cyberspace, we should take into consideration further individual, social, psychological, and also technical variables. In the case of migration biographies that can have very different individual manifestations, a qualitative approach makes sense. The function of virtual diasporas has already been copiously studied (e.g. Alonso & Oiarzabal, 2010). The question of how a regular and frequent virtual language contact with a diaspora or friends in the home country affects language development and integration in the long run still remains to be investigated in longitudinal studies.

In the case of M., a very important fact is the attitude of the husband, who does not allow his family to use Facebook. M.'s attitude towards the new media and their influence on language use is rather negative and conservative. She thinks that the very strict system of using three different registers of politeness in Korean will slowly be undermined by the way language is used in the new media. A detailed description of the Korean forms of politeness can be found in Lee Nam-Seok (1996).

Interviewer: Does the more informal style used by the young people also appear in face-to-face communication?

00:28:30
M.: That's a little bit different. That's actually somewhat different. But for the spoken language I notice that, how can I say, if it should remain formal and they shouldn't write like this in a relationship that is not so close, they try to sneak it in – not complete phrases but just a little bit.
Interviewer: And face-to-face, would they try that as well?
M.: No, no, no, this is quite rare. It is still stricter than writing an email or sms.
Interviewer: Has your own style changed?
M.: No, not me, I am still very, very conservative because I don't like it when I read blogs or where the young people write their posts, Twitter, no, not Twitter, how do you call it, blogs.
[...] Yeah, exactly, exactly, I really don't like it. And the orthography is pretty much gone, and then all the abbreviations, which I cannot understand at all. Yes, my way of writing hasn't changed with the Internet.

The expression 'they try to sneak it in' imputes a conscious and voluntary action against the dominant norms by the young people. This is a typical argument in the conflict between generations. F. also mentions the different use of language on the Internet by her younger sister. She uses the so-called Mars Language, which is characterized especially by abbreviations. When it comes to M., she expresses her normative attitude in other parts of the interview as well. She explains that she very carefully checks every email in Korean addressed to her new Korean acquaintances in Austria. 'I am not allowed to make any mistakes because I am new here' (42:02). M. is checking the emails mainly to avoid interferences from German. She is afraid of using a German style that is too direct, because she observed that the Korean diaspora in Austria is more conservative than the Korean diaspora in Germany (43:14). Emails in German to German friends are not checked. M. thinks that interferences from Korean, like the use of indirect style, will not bother the Germans. All of the interviewees declare that controlling the register is much more complex and involved with regard to a high-context culture, in this case the Korean, Filipino, and Taiwanese culture, than with regard to the low-context German culture. Like M., L. also distinguishes very carefully between the different diaspora communities. Filipinos living in the USA communicate in a different way to Filipinos living in Manila, even if they communicate in Taglish.

This section makes clear how M. constitutes her identity as a Korean in Germany as language practice, even in virtual communication, in a process of approach and acquisition as well as rejection. Crispin Thurlow, Laura Lengel, and Alice Tomic (2007) point to the influence of the ideological climate in which we are raised and in which we live on our identity construction: 'As such, we have to recognize the powerful influence of dominant ideologies in controlling and sustaining people's sense of themselves. Dominant ideologies impose their own norms and rules' (p. 98). This also holds true for identity construction on the Internet, as can be seen in all examples, with the limitation that the Internet offers us at random many different environments. The interview excerpt, however, likewise shows that identity construction cannot be regarded as separate from the users' non-virtual life situation since the non-virtual and the virtual normative systems and ideologies inform one another. Crispin Thurlow and Kristine Mroczek (2011) identify for new media sociolinguistics the following organizing principles: 'discourse, technology, multimodality, ideology'

(p. 1). The overlapping areas between virtual and non-virtual environments can be made clear in a problem-centered interview.

Conclusion

Excerpts from the three in-depth interviews illustrate that it is possible to record central issues and questions of CMC with the help of the in-depth interview as an instrument for intercultural research. The interculturality of the research process itself as an interactive process of negotiation of different meanings leads to a process of mutual awareness. It is true for the entire interview situation, as noted by Jan Blommaert and Dong Jie (2010):

> Let us keep this motto in mind. People are not cultural or linguistic catalogues, and most of what we see as their cultural and social behaviour is performed without reflecting on it and without an active awareness that is actually something they do. (p. 3)

Within this research process, it is quite possible that misunderstandings are not uncovered *in situ*, but only in the analysis of the data. Thus, it would be ideal if the interview partners could also be involved in evaluating the data. Such procedures, however, have not yet explicitly been developed in intercultural research.

In all of the three interviews, central sociolinguistic and intercultural categories become pertinent and are discussed in intercultural research literature. L. handles attribution of cultural categories with much care. F. clearly ascribes the misunderstanding she reports to the use of different politeness registers. M. ascribes subversive intentions to the young users in softening politeness conventions in Korean. For all three interviewees, it was obvious that they had to check the registers they use in relation to their communication partners. However, their controlling strategies are varied. They all think that the adjustment to a high-context culture is more demanding, even if they write in their native language. Especially F. describes the difficulty of dealing with the high speed with which she has to change from one culturally determined routine to another. This is one important aspect of the higher frequency of interpenetration as defined by Hongladarom. The attitude to the media is also very decisive. L. and F. spent an important part of their social life in the social networks. M. has developed a normative and conservative attitude as a resistance to interpenetration.

It might be useful to distinguish push-and-pull factors for cultural interpenetration through virtual communication. Long-time observations would be very interesting. Hongladarom is probably right only to a certain extent. There is a very important impact of processes of conscious and unconscious interpenetration. However, there are also very conscious processes of controlling these interpenetrations by linguistic and stylistic means. For this, culture change can only be in part considered a natural process. The Internet and particularly the social networks open a space to cultural and linguistic change. But in the end, the users decide freely if they will permit interpenetration or not – if they will share values or not – if they create different platforms for different friends from different cultures or not – if they adopt the 'Mars Languages' or remain conservative, if they write in one, two, three languages or even in a mixed one, who they invite to their platforms, and so on … The code in intercultural virtual communication is not fixed. It is negotiated! On a micro-level of communication, this is a very democratic basis for equity. Following the ethical aspirations of Cheong et al., intercultural CMC research must continue to develop methodologically, in order to do justice to this dynamics and diversity, and to help mirror this diversity even in research.

References

Alonso, A., & Oiarzabal, P.J. (2010). *Diasporas in the new media age. Identity, politics and community.* Reno: University of Nevada Press.

Alpermann, B. (2012). Qualitative Interviewforschung in China [Qualitative research with interviews in China]. In J. Kruse, S. Bethmann, D. Niermann, & Ch. Schmieder (Eds.), *Qualitative Interviewforschung in und mit fremden Sprachen* [Interviews in qualitative research in and with foreign languages] (pp. 165–185). Weinheim: Beltz Juventa.

Baker, W. (2011). Intercultural awareness: Modeling an understanding of cultures in intercultural communication through English as a lingua franca. *Language and Intercultural Communication, 11*(3), 197–214.

Baron, N.S. (2008). *Always on. Language in an online and mobile world.* Oxford: Oxford University Press.

Beer, B. (2007). Interviews. In J. Straub, A. Weidemann, & D. Weidemann (Eds.), *Handbuch interkulturelle Kommunikation und Kompetenz* [Handbook intercultural communication and competence] (pp. 334–341). Stuttgart, Weimar: J.B. Metzler.

Blommaert, J., & Jie, D. (2010). *Ethnographic fieldwork. A beginner's guide.* Bristol: Multilingual Matters.

Cassell, J., & Tversky, D. (2005). The language of online intercultural community formation. *Journal of Computer-Mediated Communication, 10*(2), article 2. Retrieved from http://jcmc.indiana.edu/vol10/issue2/cassell.html

Cheong, P.H., Martin, J.N., & Macfadyen, L.P. (Eds.). (2012). *New media and intercultural communication. Identity, community and politics.* New York: Peter Lang.

Crystal, D. (2006). *Language and the Internet* (2nd ed.). Cambridge: Cambridge University Press.

Fetscher, D. (2009). 'Multi-voicedness' in internet guest-books of German and Italian teenagers. *Language and Intercultural Communication, 9,* 33–42.

Fetscher, D. (2010). Virtual classrooms. In A. Weidemann, J. Straub, & S. Nothnagel (Eds.), *Wie lehrt man interkulturelle Kompetenz? Theorien, Methoden und Praxis in der Hochschulausbildung* [How to teach intercultural competence? Theories and methods in high school teaching] (pp. 417–432). Bielefeld: transcript.

Gevorgyan, G., & Manucharova, N. (2009). Does culturally adapted online communication work? A study of American and Chinese Internet users' attitudes and preferences toward culturally customized web design elements. *Journal of Computer-Mediated Communication, 14*(2), 393–413. doi:10.1111/j.1083-6101.2009.01446.x/pdf

Günthner, S. (1993). *Diskursstrategien in der Interkulturellen Kommunikation. Analysen deutsch–chinesischer Gespräche* [Discourse strategies in intercultural communication. Analysis of German–Chinese conversations]. Tübingen: Niemeyer.

Haslett, B.B. (2012). A structurational interaction approach to investigating culture, identity, and mediated communication. In P.H. Cheong, J.N. Martin, & L.P. Macfadyen (Eds.), *New media and intercultural communication. Identity, community and politics.* New York: Peter Lang.

Hennig, E.-V. (2012). Verfahren der Erhebung, Evaluation und Didaktisierung von Critical Incidents [Methods of data collection, evaluation and pedagogical use of critical incidents]. In A. Schumann (Ed.), *Interkulturelle Kommunikation in der Hochschule* [Intercultural communication in the university] (pp. 81–106). Bielefeld: transcript.

Heringer, H.J. (2004). *Interkulturelle Kommunikation* [Intercultural communication]. Tübingen: A. Francke.

Hettlage-Varjas, A., & Hettlage, R. (1984). Kulturelle Zwischenwelten. Fremdarbeiter – eine Ethnie? [Immigrant workers in between the cultures – An ethnie?]. *Schweizerische Zeitschrift für Soziologie, 10*(2), 357–405.

Hongladarom, S. (n.d.). *On the Internet and cultural differences.* Retrieved from http://homepage.mac.com/soraj/web/Internet.pdf

Knoblauch, H., & Kotthoff, H. (Eds.). (2001). *Verbal art across cultures.* Tübingen: Gunter Narr.

Kotthoff, H. (2009). Ritual and style across cultures. In H. Kotthoff & H. Spencer-Oaty (Eds.) *Handbook of intercultural communication* (pp. 173–197). Berlin: Mouton de Gruyter.

Kruse, J., Bethmann, S., Niermann, D., & Schmieder, Ch. (2012). *Qualitative Interviewforschung in und mit fremden Sprachen* [Interviewing in qualitative research in and with foreign languages]. Weinheim: Beltz Juventa.

Kvale, S., & Brinkmann, S. (2009). *Interviews. Learning the craft of qualitative research interviewing* (2nd ed.). Los Angeles, CA: Sage.

Lazar, J., Feng, J.H., & Hochheiser, H. (2010). *Research methods in human–computer interaction.* Chichester: Wiley.

Lee, J. (2012). Rite of death as a popular commodity: Neoliberalism, media, and New Korean funeral culture. In P.H. Cheong, J.N. Martin, & L.P. Macfadyen (Eds.), *New media and intercultural communication. Identity, community and politics* (pp. 175–191). New York: Peter Lang.

Lee, N.-S. (1996). *Deixis und Honorifika. Allgemeine deiktische Phänomene und die pragmatische Komponente des Koreanischen* [Deixis and Honorifika. General deictical phenomena and the pragmatic component of Korean]. Tübingen: Gunter Narr.

Leppänen, S., Pitkänen-Huhta, A., Piirainen-Marsh, A., Nikula, T., & Peuronen, S. (2009). Young people's translocal new media uses: A multiperspective analysis of language choice and heteroglossia. *Journal of Computer-Mediated Communication, 14,* 1080–1107. doi:10.1111/j.1083-6101.2009.01482.x

Przyborski, A., & Wohlrab-Sahr, M. (2008). *Qualitative Sozialforschung. Ein Arbeitsbuch* [Qualitative research. A workbook]. München: Oldenbourg Wissenschaftsverlag GmbH.

Roberts, K.G. (2008). Dialogic ethics, cosmopolitanism, and intercultural communication. In K.G. Roberts & R.C. Arnett (Eds.), *Communication ethics. Between cosmopolitanism and provinciality* (pp. 89–104). New York: Peter Lang.

Schröer, N. (2009). *Interkulturelle Kommunikation. Einführung* [Intercultural communication. Introduction]. Essen: Oldib.

Shuter, R. (2012). When Indian women text message: Culture, identity, and emerging interpersonal norms of new media. In P.H. Cheong, J.N. Martin, & L.P. Macfadyen (Eds.), *New media and intercultural communication. Identity, community and politics* (pp. 209–221). New York: Peter Lang.

Thompson, R.M. (2003). *Filipino English and Taglish. Language switching from multiple perspectives.* Amsterdam: John Benjamins.

Thurlow, C., Lengel, L., & Tomic, A. (2007). *Computer mediated communication* (2nd ed.). Los Angeles, CA: Sage.

Thurlow, C., & Mroczek, K. (2011). Introduction: Fresh perspectives on new media sociolinguistics. In C. Thurlow & K. Mroczek (Eds.), *Digital discourse: Language in the new media* (pp. xiv–xliv). New York: Oxford University Press.

Witzel, A. (2000). Das problemzentrierte Interview [The focused interview]. *Forum Qualitative Sozialforschung, 1*(1), article 22. Retrieved from http://www.qualitative-research.net/index.php/fqs/article/viewArticle/1132/2519

Are you an ELF? The relevance of ELF as an equitable social category in online intercultural communication

Christopher Jenks

Department of English, City University of Hong Kong, Hong Kong

This paper examines the different social categories that are made relevant when geographically dispersed speakers of English as an additional language communicate in chat rooms. Although the literature characterizes these interactions as English as a lingua franca, this paper explores to what extent interactants see themselves as lingua franca speakers. Membership categorization analysis is used to investigate how social categories related to English are enacted in, and through, talk and interaction. This is done by investigating language proficiency compliments, talk of language proficiency, and getting acquainted sequences. While English is the medium of communication in these chat rooms, the findings reveal that English as a lingua franca is not a social category that is made relevant during talk. When constructing identities in relation to English, the social categories that are made relevant are foreigner, language learner, and non-native. These observations are then used to argue that an equitable, impartial, and context-sensitive approach to examining identities in intercultural communication requires abandoning the more traditional method of ascribing social categories a priori. The paper ends by exploring the validity of using the term English as a lingua franca when interactants possess, and make relevant, a number of different social categories when speaking in English.

本文考察了不同國家或地區以英語為第二語言使用者在網絡英語聊天室里聊天所涉及的不同社會類別。以往的研究將在此類交流歸類於英語作為通用語的交流,而本文則旨在探討在多大程度上這些聊天者認為自己是英語作為通用語的使用者。本文採用會員分類分析來研究聊天室交流中英語使用所涉及的社會類別。具體研究方法包括分析談話過程中聊天者對對方英語語言程度的讚美和討論,以及互相自我介紹和認識的談話順序。在這些聊天室里雖然英語是溝通媒介,調查結果卻顯示英語作為通用語并不是聊天過程中非常相關的一個社會類別。在建構與英語相關的身份認同時,所涉及的社會類別為: 外國人, 語言學習者和非本族語者。本研究中觀察結果顯示, 如果以一個公平、 客觀以及重視語境的研究方法來研究在跨文化交際中的身份認同則應該摒棄傳統研究方法中社會類別先入為主的觀念。文章最後探討了聊天者在聊天中使用"英語作為通用語"這 一術語的合理性以及聊天者在使用英語時的其它相關的社會類別。

Introduction

Social categories – for example, female, student, and American – play an important role in applied linguistics research (Sealey & Carter, 2004). They are used to categorize, and therefore investigate, members of society, and thus provide a descriptive framework for understanding how people make sense of each other and their surroundings. Social categories are also used to understand how interactants co-construct identities (Antaki & Widdicombe, 1998), examine whether membership to a cultural group is associated with specific grammatical features (Whitehead & Lerner, 2009), and make critical observations pertaining to relations of power (Morgan, 2010).

Researchers use one of two approaches in the study of social categories: deductive and inductive. The deductive approach involves categorizing interactants before (and sometimes without) examining whether the social category has relevance to the interactions under investigation (e.g. whether research participants tropicalize the identities ascribed to them by the researcher). The deductive approach is highly positivistic, as evidenced by the many sociolinguistics studies that use social categories as independent variables: social categories are used to measure whether pre-defined group(s) of people exhibit particular linguistic and/or interactional behaviors.

The inductive approach entails categorizing interactants according to how and what social categories are constructed in communication. The inductive approach produces analytic descriptions based on the understanding that social categories must be problematized; that is, this approach does not take for granted the fluid nature of social categories. The underpinning thought here is that interactants have a great degree of 'say' (or agency) in identity construction. To borrow a term from the positivistic tradition, social categories are 'dependent' variables.

The methodological differences that exist between deductive and inductive approaches are not new to applied linguistics (see Benwell & Stokoe, 2006), but the issue of how to investigate social categories is nonetheless integral to the development of the discipline in key areas of research. One such area of research that will be discussed in this paper is globalization. Simply put, globalization is the interconnectedness that exists in the world (Giddens, 1990). With regard to increased interconnectedness, communication technologies are an important catalyst for globalization. As a result of technological advancements and growth in online media consumption, societies are more mobile and interconnected now than ever before. People can easily communicate across time and space, and with little delay. Current trends in (online) communication have forced researchers to re-examine existing understandings of what it means to be an English speaker in a globalized world. For example, what does it mean to be a lingua franca speaker of English?

This study examines what social categories are made relevant when interactants communicate in a 'global' context. While there are many social categories that are associated with speaking English (e.g. native versus non-native, immigrant versus citizen, local versus outsider, language user versus language learner), the discussion below begins with the two social categories that are perhaps the most widely used in applied linguistics research: English as a foreign language (EFL) speaker and English as lingua franca (ELF) speaker.

The aim of the paper is to examine what and how social categories are made relevant when geographically dispersed speakers of English as an additional language communicate in online voice-based chat rooms. These interactions are often characterized as ELF (Jenkins, 2007), as the speakers do not share a common first language. Rather than assume that ELF is of relevance to the interactions and interactants examined in this study, this paper explores to what extent people see themselves as ELF speakers.

Membership categorization analysis is used to investigate what and how English language social categories are enacted in, and through, talk and interaction. This issue is addressed by investigating language proficiency compliments, talk of language proficiency, and getting acquainted sequences. These interactional episodes are typically organized around the discussion of social categories, and thus lend themselves to an investigation of English language identities. The findings are then used to put forward the argument that an equitable, impartial, and context-sensitive approach to examining identities in intercultural communication research requires abandoning the more traditional method of ascribing social categories a priori. The paper ends by exploring the ethics of using the term ELF when interactants possess, and make relevant, a number of different social categories when speaking in English.

EFL versus ELF

Many social categories are used in descriptions of, and discussions pertaining to, speakers of English, as discussed in the introductory section. The two that are particularly germane to the present study are EFL and ELF. Although EFL and ELF are commonly used to describe the same people and communicative settings, these social categories are associated with different theoretical positions. Before uncovering how speakers enact social categories in English language encounters, and exploring what can be gleaned from such an analysis, it is important to review what these two terms mean and identify how they are used in the literature.

The term EFL defines settings where English is not used as an official (or main) language, and is commonly used to characterize, and distinguish between, teaching and learning situations (cf. EFL teaching or EFL learning). EFL is also used to characterize the people that belong to such settings: a teacher and learner are referred to as EFL teacher and EFL learner, respectively. The term EFL allows researchers to discuss their observations and findings in relation to specific contextual issues – to compare, for example, the pedagogical differences between foreign language and second language settings.

Notwithstanding the descriptive problems in using EFL to characterize entire regions and nation-states,[1] the term is informed by several contextual assumptions that are important to a discussion of social categories. These assumptions are important, as they form part of the discourse that is used in the literature to ascribe and construct identities in relation to English.

A common assumption is that while English is valued in EFL settings, the people of these regions and nation-states do not have many opportunities to use English outside of classrooms. English is not used in everyday communication, and so speakers have few, if any at all, opportunities to use the language in naturally occurring communicative situations. In such settings, English examinations are integral to the long-term academic and professional development of students.[2] High scores on English examinations give students the competitive edge when seeking admission into university and applying for work after higher education. These contextual assumptions, or realities for many regions and nation-states, shape the ways in which English is used. For example, in the EFL classroom, tests often dictate what is taught, and grammar is typically given priority over conversational skills.[3]

Because socio-political histories determine what 'regional' English will be taught, and thus used in EFL settings (e.g. the socio-political history of the USA and South Korea means that American English is currently the most commonly taught English in South Korea), teachers and students have ostensibly little say in what is 'right' and 'wrong' with regard to English language usage. Teachers have little say in that they must teach in a way that will enable students to score well on tests and meet societal expectations of what is 'good' English. This often requires teachers to conform to a particular – and often narrow – set of assumptions with regard to English language usage. Tests are based on non-local standards (Shohamy, 2001), and many people believe that speaking 'good' English amounts to mimicking American or British conventions. As a result, teachers (and society in general) place less value on sounding, say, Korean when speaking English. Put differently, the local use of English outside of classrooms is rarely taken into consideration when teaching EFL.

While the contextual variables identified above continue to shape the teaching and learning of English in multiple regions and nation-states, many applied researchers question the utility in using terms like foreign and non-native in an increasingly globalized world (Canagarajah, 2006; Firth, 2009; Widdowson, 1994, 1997). For example, some researchers argue that such terms imply that using English amounts to being a foreigner (Firth & Wagner, 1997): EFL is not about local identities and practices, but conforming to the standards that have been determined by a small set of regions and nation-states (cf. Interlanguage Theory; Selinker, 1992). It is often argued that because standards are not localized, deviations from American or British English are seen as non-American or non-British features of English. That is, deviations are seen as deficiencies in, or features of 'foreign' or 'bad,' English.

The criticisms that have been made of EFL have led to calls for a more global, context-sensitive understanding of diversity in English language use. The move away from the allegedly ethnocentric models of English has led to growth in several areas of study, including ELF. Scholars working in this area of study argue – and indeed are informed by the principle – that observations of, and discussions pertaining to, speakers of English must reflect the contextual realities of using English in an interconnected world – for example, the fact that speakers of English as an additional language far outnumber those that speak English as a first (and often only) language (Graddol, 2006).

ELF is commonly defined as a contact language used by speakers of English as an additional language that do not share a common mother tongue (Jenkins, 2007). As with the term EFL, ELF is used to describe and characterize interactions and interactants. In international business meetings, for example, the language and participants of such settings are referred to as ELF interaction and ELF speakers, respectively (e.g. Pullin, 2010, p. 457).

Further examples of researchers using ELF as a social category include the observation that speakers in lingua franca encounters omit third person singular and the pluralization of uncountable nouns (see Seidlhofer, 2004), the characterization that lingua franca interactants are socially and linguistically mutually supportive (Meierkord, 2000), which results in overlooking ungrammatical and unidiomatic constructions (cf. 'let-it-pass' principle; see Firth, 1996),[4] and most notably, Jenkins' finding that ELF possesses core phonological properties (2000).

In addition to being helpful in generating analytic descriptions of interactions and interactants in new and emerging settings, the term ELF is used to critically evaluate teaching and learning theories and practices. For instance, Jenkins (2000) believes that the core phonological properties of ELF should inform the teaching and learning of English pronunciation in EFL regions and nation-states (for similar observations, see Jenkins, 2006a, 2006b; Seidlhofer, 2004). This argument is partly based on the belief that English 'is no longer viewed as connected to the culture of the traditional English-dominant countries' (Baker, 2009, p. 570), and that ELF speakers are 'international' or 'global' stakeholders of English (Meierkord, 2002).

Despite the empirical and pedagogical contributions made as a result of examining lingua franca interactions, perceptions of, values placed on, and purposes for using English, vary so greatly from one context to another that the term ELF has the potential to become a blunt or clumsy analytic tool – the same can be, and has been, said for using EFL to characterize entire regions and nation-states (Firth & Wagner, 1997). From a descriptive standpoint, the term loses a high degree of validity when used with little attention to whether ELF is relevant to the interactants and interactions under investigation.

Thus, in order to produce equitable and context-sensitive analytic descriptions, researchers must not blindly or precipitously assume that the terms used in their studies – be that EFL or ELF – reflect the social realities of research participants. Demonstrating that social categories and analytic descriptions are somehow representations of social realities requires a data-driven, bottom-up approach. The following section identifies and explicates the approach used in this study.

The study

The findings reported below stem from approximately eight hours of data. This data set comes from a much larger corpus of multi-party voice-based chat room interactions (see Jenks, 2009). Most of the chat room participants are speakers of English as an additional language. The interactants come from many regions and nation-states, including Korea, Japan, Turkey, and Egypt. Screen names are used for all extracts presented below. English is the medium of communication in all of the chat rooms. Many of the titles given to the chat rooms reflect a preference to speak English (e.g. 'English-Only Chat Room'), though on many occasions throughout the data set, interactants would switch to and from different languages.

Although the interactions that take place in these chat rooms can be characterized as ELF (cf. Jenkins, 2007), this paper examines whether this social category is interactionally relevant for the interactants under investigation. The purpose for doing so is threefold: (1) to investigate how interactants construct identities in relation to English, (2) to explore whether ELF is a social category that is used during lingua franca encounters, and (3) to discuss these findings in relation to ethics and equity.

The methodology used to do this is membership categorization analysis (henceforth, MCA). The analytic aim of MCA is to examine the discursive construction of social categories (for a detailed discussion of how MCA can be employed to investigate intercultural interactions, see Jenks, 2012). The utility in using MCA is that it allows researchers to show how social categories are made relevant through interactional conduct. For example, correcting a grammatical mistake can be treated as an invocation of an expert identity. In the context of this study, a language proficiency compliment can be used to co-construct identities related to being a speaker of English. In MCA, social categories are believed to be situated in, and co-constructed through, talk and interaction. Put differently, MCA researchers do not assume that social categories are constructed outside of the context in which communication occurs. In practice, this means that MCA researchers do not ascribe social categories to research participants before meticulously examining the discourse under investigation.

Unlike other discourse analytic approaches, MCA is based on the principle that observations of social categories must be shown to be demonstrably relevant, and procedurally consequential, for the talk and talk-based activities at hand (Sacks, 1992). The issue of relevance and procedural consequentiality is underpinned by the idea that social realities – for example, the identity of being a language learner – are an interactional achievement (Schegloff, 2007). For instance, the practice of evaluating linguistic competence may create the possibility to discuss identities related to being a learner, but in order for this possibility to be borne out, the recipient of the compliment must use this social category in the response turn. Similarly, talk about food-eating practices can create opportunities to discuss, and therefore make relevant, national identities, but this is something that is jointly produced as interaction unfolds (Brandt & Jenks, 2011). The upshot is that a priori assumptions of what is and what is not relevant with regard to social categories are not made when using MCA. Researchers must situate their analytic descriptions and observations of social categories in the turn-by-turn moments of interaction. Thus, analytic descriptions and observations are based on transcripts of talk and interaction that detail the intricate ways in which talk and interaction are managed.

Findings

Three extracts are examined in this section. These three extracts show the type of interactional work that is prototypically involved in co-constructing identities related to being a speaker of English. In each of the following extracts, and indeed the larger data set that informs the analysis here, interactants use their English language identities to manage talk in the chat room. Although the participants belong to a number of different social categories, including lingua franca speaker, the examples below show that when opportunities are given to discuss English language identities, categories related to being a learner or non-native speaker are made relevant.

In the first example, several interactants are discussing the topic of singing. The extract begins with Winnie's complimenting Roci's voice (for transcription conventions, see Appendix).

(1)
1h - 13:42-14:05
```
1   Winnie:     no you got a rea↑lly↓ be:autiful voice.
2               you should be a dee↑[jay↓ sometime.
3   Roci:                           [yeah↓
4               (1.0)
5   Roci:       u:h no↓ you know uh- i may- i- i- even tried
6               to work at a call center here. (.) in the
7               philippines but↑ you know↓ (0.4) they think
8               that my english is not yet too good so↓ i↑
9               was↓ not↑ hired↓
10  Winnie:     no it's pretty good t[o me.
11  Roci:                            [yeah
12              (1.0)
13  Roci:       alright thank you for that you↑ know↓ because
14              i have been practicing it here. i::n skype↓
```

The identity work in this example begins in lines 1 and 2, when Winnie compliments Roci's voice and states that he should be a DJ. While this initiates the identity work that occurs later in the extract, the turn itself does not display any orientation to English language identities.

That is, Winnie's turn does not contain any social categories that are explicitly linked to the status of being an English speaker. Winnie does not say 'you have a beautiful English voice' or 'you should be an English DJ.' In other words, possessing a good voice to sing (or DJ) could be associated with any language. Furthermore, the practice of complimenting is not associated with any specific identity. In a language classroom, for example, the practice of complimenting someone's voice is not tied to an institutional role (e.g. teacher or student).

Although there is nothing explicitly in, and about, Winnie's turn that demonstrates that she is engaging in identity work, Roci responds to the compliment by making relevant his status as a speaker of English (lines 5–9). This is done when Roci identifies a past situation where he was not hired because of his English language abilities. In so doing, Roci topicalizes, and thus makes relevant, his proficiency in English.

In line 10, Winnie disagrees with the previous turn and provides a second compliment. Here Winnie refers specifically to Roci's ability to use English, as it follows his account of when he was not hired because of his language proficiency. In providing a language proficiency compliment, Roci's ability to use English becomes procedurally consequential to the talk at hand. In lines 13 and 14, Roci accepts the language proficiency compliment, and states that his English is commendable because he has been practicing it.

In this exchange, Roci's English language identity is made relevant in several instances. The first instance occurs when Roci uses his English language identity to disagree with Winnie's first compliment. In the second instance, Winnie provides a language proficiency compliment, thereby making relevant Roci's English language identity. Language proficiency compliments are particularly important to an understanding of identity work, as compliment recipients often respond by using, or making reference to, social categories (Jenks, in press). This is in fact what happens in the above exchange: the third instance occurs when Roci responds to the language proficiency compliment. Here Roci accepts the compliment by stating that he practices English. The practice of practicing (a language) is often associated with specific social categories. Practicing it is not, for instance, associated with teachers or the act of teaching. It would be highly unusual for a teacher to state that she is practicing English. Conversely, practicing a language is often associated with learners and the act of learning.

From a descriptive standpoint, what social category best captures Roci's English language identity? In other words, what social category should be used to characterize this speaker? Roci is speaking English, and in several instances makes relevant his English language identity. Roci does not refer to himself as an ELF speaker, nor does he refer to the social categories that are often associated with this identity (e.g. world English speaker or global speaker of English). Although Roci does not explicitly refer to himself as a learner, he does use a social category that is often associated with being a learner. Before exploring these issues further, a second example will be introduced and analyzed for further discussion.

The second example takes place in a different chat room. Young and Sayed are discussing the topic of travel. After several minutes of discussion, Young switches topics, and asks whether Sayed should be in school. The extract begins with Young's question.

```
(2)
1d - 19:51-20:50
1                    (1.2)
2    Young:          aren't you↓ supposed↑ to be at
3                    school, (0.6) no?
4                    (1.4)
5    Sayed:          yeah i- i- yeah you're right but this
6                    semester i:: (.) i didn't attend eh::
7                    university (0.5) i go↓ back↑ the next
8                    semester.
9                    (0.8)
10   Young:          ah::: okay↓ (1.1) okay i↑ see↓ =
11   Sayed:          =yeah (0.4) so i'm spending my time
12                   on skypecast.
13                   (0.4)
14   Young:          mmhm=
15   Sayed:          =improving my english
16                   (0.3)
17   Young:          >your english really good though> (.)
18                   <°i think.° <
19                   (1.8)
20   Sayed:          no- no s- s- som- somehow when i talk
21                   to (0.6) native speakers (0.2) i::: have↓
22                   to↑ re:peat↓ my sentences my- many times
23                   (0.5) they can't da- they- uh- they do not
24                   understand many of my words (0.8) my- i- i-
25                   i mean my pronunciation is not that good.
26                   (1.4)
27   Young:          but i ca- o::h i can understand you maybe
28                   i'm not a n(hh)ative speaker m(hh)aybe (0.2)
29                   i don't know.hhh (0.2) but uh- (.) you're:
30                   english [is pretty good↓ i↑ think↓
31   Sayed:                  [yes be- yeah because we have two
32                   foreigners
33   Young:          ok↑ay↓ i↑ see↓
```

Young's question in lines 2 and 3 leads to a series of responses that initiate the identity work that takes place in this exchange. In lines 5–8, Sayed acknowledges the fact that he should be in school ('yeah you're right'), and later in lines 11 and 12, identifies what he has been doing in lieu of university studies ('i'm spending my time on skypecast'). In line 15, Sayed completes his extended turn to Young's question by identifying the reason why he is spending his time online ('improving my english').

Sayed's reason for chatting online is noteworthy. As with the social practice of practicing English (cf. Extract 1, line 14), 'improving' is an act that is associated with specific social categories. For example, it would be highly unusual for a monolingual speaker to state that she is improving her English. Conversely, the practice of improving language proficiency is often associated with students, or learners.

The practice of improving also implies that an interactant's language proficiency is not at a desired level. This is in fact how Young treats the previous turn. In line 17, she provides a language proficiency compliment ('your english really good though'), a response typically given to negative self-appraisals. Although Sayed could change topics by simply accepting the positive appraisal, he uses the compliment to prolong the discussion of identities.

In lines 20–25, Sayed responds to the compliment by disagreeing and stating that native speakers do not understand him well. The identity work involved in these turns is particularly significant with regard to English language identities. Sayed's response here shifts the focus from being a speaker that lacks a desired level of proficiency to an interactant that does not belong to the native speaker community ('they do not understand'). Sayed then completes his turn with a negative assessment of his pronunciation ('my pronunciation is not that good').

As with the first negative self-appraisal, Young responds to Sayed by stating that his English is at an acceptable level. However, Young qualifies her positive appraisal by stating that she is not a native speaker ('i'm not a native speaker'). In so doing, the issue of being or not being a native speaker becomes procedurally consequential to the talk at hand. The status of being a native speaker of English is made relevant in further talk in lines 31 and 32, where Sayed states that the reason why Young can understand him is because they are both 'foreigners.'

As with Extract 1, the interactants in Extract 2 are speaking English as an additional language and do not share a common mother tongue. Moreover, the interactants are highly proficient in that they can discuss complex topics in a fluid and unstilted manner. In other words, the interactants belong to a number of different social categories related to being a speaker of English (e.g. expert speaker of English, world English speaker, lingua franca speaker). Despite this fact, the interactants see themselves as learners and non-native speakers of English when discussing topics related to English. In other words, the interactants do not see themselves as experts or lingua franca speakers of English, or at least these social categories are not made relevant, when engaging in talk during lingua franca encounters. Given these observations, what social category should be used to characterize these speakers?

Before addressing this analytic conundrum, a final extract is presented. The third example is taken from a chat room where several interactants are discussing places of residence. Roci has just learnt that Jin is a South Korean living in England with her American husband. The exchange begins with Roci asking Jin whether looking for a job is difficult.

(3)
1h - 04:18-04:42
```
1   Roci:      uh:: eh- is- is looking for a you know
2              job  [uh::
3   Jin:            [mm↑hm↓
4   Roci:      difficult for- for you as a newcomer.
5              (0.7)
6   Jin:       .hh ye[s↓
7   Roci:            [(even though) your your husband is
8              an american
9              (.)
```

```
10  Jin:    uh::[: ye::
11  Roci:        [you↑ know↓
12  Jin:    yes↓ but- but he works at a university
13           he teaches you↑ know↓ at school but↑ uh↓
14           (.) tsk .hhh you know i: taught english in
15           korea but i can't teach english in the
16           u↑k↓ (.) because i'm not↑ a↓ you↑ know↓
17           (0.2) u[h::
18  Roci:          [yeah.
19           (.)
20  Roci:    n[ative speaker
21  Jin:      [native speaker (.) i'm not a native
22           speaker
```

The identity work that takes place in this exchange occurs with Jin's turn in line 12. This turn begins with a 'yes,' though it is not entirely clear whether Jin is agreeing with Roci's assumption that it is difficult to find employment in the UK or the fact that her husband is an American (or indeed, if she is simply providing a verbal receipt of the question). In lines 12 and 13, Jin continues with her response by stating that her husband teaches, but later switches the focus to her ('i taught english in korea'). Jin's announcement is followed by the assertion that she cannot pursue teaching in the UK because she is not a native speaker ('i'm not a native speaker').

Jin's extended turn reveals a great deal about the type of identity work that takes place in these chat rooms. In one part of her turn, Jin refers to herself as a language teacher (lines 14 and 15). In a different part of her turn (lines 21 and 22), Jin refers to herself as a non-native speaker. In making the distinction between teaching English in Korea and the UK, Jin relativizes her English language identity. Although Jin is an English language teacher in her home country, her status as a non-native speaker does not allow her to teach English in the UK.

As with all of the extracts examined in this section, practices and social categories associated with being a student, learner, and/or non-native speaker are referred to and used when managing talk in chat rooms. This occurs despite the fact that the interactants belong to a number of different social categories. For example, in Extract 3, despite Jin's status as a highly proficient speaker of English, it is her 'non-nativeness' that is made relevant when accounting for issues related to living and working in the UK.

Given the analytic observations provided for Extracts 1–3, what social category should be used when describing the interactants of this study? Do researchers have an obligation to use categories, such as ELF or world English speaker, as these social categories are underpinned by the idea that linguistic variation and local conventions are important aspects of using English? Alternatively, should academics refrain from using social categories that research participants do not perceive to be relevant (e.g. ELF speaker), especially if the alternatives are deemed to be ethnocentric (e.g. EFL speaker)? The discussion in the following section explores these ethical issues in more detail.

Discussion and conclusion

Researchers make a number of important decisions when conceptualizing, carrying out, and writing up research on intercultural communication. Researchers select theoretical frameworks, determine the best data collection tools to use, and weigh the benefits and disadvantages of different methodologies, to name a few. Researchers also make decisions based on ethical considerations. For example, ethical issues are often guiding factors when collecting, transcribing, and presenting data recordings. Decisions must be made regarding anonymity, the use of pseudonyms, and the ethical implications of such actions.

This is no different when conducting research in settings where English is used as an additional language. In addition to making decisions based on the aforementioned issues, researchers must also decide on which social categories will be used to describe and discuss the interactions and interactants under investigation. This decision is inherently theoretical and bound to the ethics of conducting research. While there are many social categories that are associated with English interactions and interactants (e.g. second language, world English, learner, expert), EFL and ELF are two of the most commonly used in studies of English as an additional language. As the discussion in the beginning of this paper has demonstrated, these two social categories represent different theoretical positions.

As such, selecting a social category to describe a group of speakers is a theoretical act. Researchers have theoretical justifications for selecting one social category over the other. While there is nothing particularly noteworthy about the idea that theory informs practice, researchers have an ethical obligation to ensure that, or at least engage in a discussion that addresses the issue of whether, social categories reflect social realities. This is because researchers have a great deal of power in how research participants are portrayed to a larger, albeit academic, audience. Therefore, selecting social categories, like choosing pseudonyms for research participants, is part of the ethics of conducting research. It is thus not enough for researchers to select social categories according to theoretical justifications. Researchers must also be reflexive when selecting social categories – they must examine to what extent social categories have social relevance to the interactions and interactants under investigation, and to explore whether alternative social categories should be used in light of such an examination.

This is what has been done in this study. Three extracts were presented to show how interactants construct identities in relation to English. The findings demonstrated that when English language identities are made relevant during online encounters, interactants see themselves, and orient to each other, as language learners, non-native speakers, and even foreigners. These social categories are made relevant despite the fact that all of the interactants are highly proficient English speakers, and speaking in a lingua franca setting. Conversely, the interactants do not see themselves as lingua franca speakers, world English speakers, or speakers of English as an international language.

Does this mean that ELF should not be used to describe the interactions and interactants of this study? On the one hand, it could be argued that it is ethically sound to use ELF, as this social category places value on local conventions and empowers speakers of English as an additional language. On the other hand, it could be argued that it is ethically sound to be faithful to the social categories that are relevant for research participants. This decision stems from the idea that if research participants come from regions where the status of being a foreign language speaker is socially and interactionally important, then they should be described as such. A discussion of the ethics of selecting social categories like this is needed in order for intercultural communication research to move forward in a world where more and more people speak English. However, the ethics of selecting social categories does not stop here.

The decision to select a social category must also be equitable with regard to how interactions and interactants are portrayed in publications. Again, this is because researchers are in a position of power when selecting social categories for descriptive purposes, whereas in most cases, research participants are not. An equitable decision requires addressing two issues: social relevance and power imbalance. An equitable social category is socially relevant to research participants. For the present study, this means identifying any disparity that exists between the social category that the researcher prefers (i.e. ELF) and the one that is made relevant in the data (i.e. EFL). An equitable social category will take into consideration any disparity that exists. This entails selecting the social category that is made relevant by the interactants, and in the interactions, under investigation. An equitable decision also addresses the imbalance of power that exists between the researcher and the researched. In addition to addressing social relevance, a researcher can counterbalance power by asking research participants how they would like to be portrayed to an academic audience. This empowers research participants by giving them some control in the research process.

With that said, however, it could be argued that researchers have an ethical obligation to dismiss social categories that negatively portray research participants, even if the issue of social relevance is not addressed. For example, the interactants investigated in this study see themselves as non-natives and foreigners. Although ELF has no social relevance to the interactions investigated in this study, the social category is linguistically useful in promoting the understanding that English is used in many ways and for varied purposes. That is, ELF moves researchers away from the ethnocentric model used by SLA researchers.

As with many issues, however, differences will always exist with regard to what is right or wrong when selecting social categories. While it is beyond the scope of this paper to comprehensively discuss the merits of EFL and ELF, the point to be taken in these discussions is that there are theoretical, political, and ethical implications for selecting social categories. Researchers must not only be aware of these implications, but they must also identify the justifications for selecting a particular social category. For example, if a researcher has clear motives for selecting ELF over EFL (for instance, the researcher wishes to be more equitable when selecting social categories), then this should be identified and discussed, and not dismissed and/or overlooked as it has been in most studies to date. At the same time, researchers have an ethical obligation to address the imbalance of power that exists in selecting social categories for descriptive purposes. Researchers can address the issue of power in many ways, from selecting social categories according to social relevance to incorporating research participants into the decision-making process. Whichever approach is taken, researchers must be more cognizant of, and discuss more explicitly, the reasons for selecting social categories. The analysis and discussion in the paper represents a small step forward, but researchers must continue to examine social categories in different contexts and settings.

Notes

1. The term EFL (as well as ESL) is often criticized for oversimplifying regional social and linguistic differences. For the present purpose, the term is simply used to discuss one way speakers of English are characterized in the literature.

2. Development here is not used in a cognitive sense, but rather the perceived occupational benefits of scoring high marks on examinations.
3. In the interest of simplicity, EFL is used synonymously with ESL. This is done because the main aim of this section is to identify the differences between study of EFL/ESL and ELF. Put differently, this section is not concerned with the contextual differences that exist between EFL and ESL.
4. However, Jenks (2012) shows that ELF interactants can, and do, engage in interactional practices that are highly unsupportive.

References

Antaki, C., & Widdicombe, S. (Eds.). (1998). *Identities in talk*. London: Sage.

Atkinson, J.M., & Heritage, J. (Eds.). (1984). *Structures of social action: Studies in conversation analysis*. Cambridge: Cambridge University Press.

Baker, W. (2009). The cultures of English as a lingua franca. *TESOL Quarterly*, *43*(4), 567–592.

Benwell, B., & Stokoe, E. (2006). *Discourse and identity*. Edinburgh: Edinburgh University Press.

Brandt, A., & Jenks, C.J. (2011). 'Is it okay to eat a dog in Korea … like China?' Assumptions of national food-eating practices in intercultural interaction. *Language and Intercultural Communication*, *11*(1), 41–58.

Canagarajah, S. (2006). Negotiating the local in English as a lingua franca. *Annual Review of Applied Linguistics*, *26*, 197–218.

Firth, A. (1996). The discursive accomplishment of normality: On conversation analysis and 'lingua franca' English. *Journal of Pragmatics*, *26*, 237–259.

Firth, A. (2009). The lingua franca factor. *Intercultural Pragmatics*, *6*(2), 147–170.

Firth, A., & Wagner, J. (1997). On discourse, communication, and (some) fundamental concepts in SLA research. *The Modern Language Journal*, *81*, 285–300.

Giddens, A. (1990). *The consequences of modernity*. Cambridge: Polity Press.

Graddol, D. (2006). *English next: Why global English may mean the end of 'English as a Foreign Language'*. London: British Council.

Jenkins, J. (2000). *The phonology of English as an international language*. Oxford: Oxford University Press.

Jenkins, J. (2006a). Current perspectives on teaching World Englishes and English as a Lingua Franca. *TESOL Quarterly*, *40*(1), 157–181.

Jenkins, J. (2006b). Points of view and blind spots: ELF and SLA. *International Journal of Applied Linguistics*, *16*(2), 137–162.

Jenkins, J. (2007). *English as a lingua franca: Attitude and identity*. Oxford: Oxford University Press.

Jenks, C.J. (2009). Getting acquainted in Skypecasts: Aspects of social organization in online chat rooms. *International Journal of Applied Linguistics*, *19*(1), 26–46.

Jenks, C.J. (2012). Doing being reprehensive: Some interactional features of English as a lingua franca. *Applied Linguistics*, *33*(4), 386–405.

Jenks, C.J. (in press). 'Your pronunciation and your accent is very excellent': Orientations of identity during compliment sequences in English as a lingua franca encounters. *Language and Intercultural Communication*.

Meierkord, C. (2000). Interpreting successful lingua franca interaction. An analysis of non-native/non-native small talk conversations in English. *Linguistik Online*, *5*(1). Retrieved October 21, 2012, from http://www.linguistik-online.com

Meierkord, C. (2002). 'Language stripped bare' or 'linguistic masala'? Culture in lingua franca communication. In K. Knapp & C. Meierkord (Eds.), *Lingua franca communication* (pp. 109–134). Frankfurt am Main, Germany: Peter Lang.

Morgan, M. (2010). The presentation of indirectness and power in everyday life. *Journal of Pragmatics, 42*, 283–291.

Pullin, P. (2010). Small talk, rapport and international communicative competence: Lessons to learn from BELF. *Journal of Business Communication, 47*(4), 455–476.

Sacks, H. (1992). *Lectures on conversation* (G. Jefferson, Ed.). (Vols. 1 & 2). Oxford: Basil Blackwell.

Schegloff, E.A. (2007). A tutorial on membership categorization. *Journal of Pragmatics, 39*, 462–482.

Sealey, A., & Carter, B. (2004). *Applied linguistics as social science*. London: Continuum.

Seidlhofer, B. (2004). Research perspectives on teaching English as a lingua franca. *Annual Review of Applied Linguistics, 24*, 209–239.

Selinker, L. (1992). *Rediscovering interlanguage*. London: Longman.

Shohamy, E. (2001). *The power of tests: A critical perspective on the uses of language tests*. New York: Longman.

Whitehead, K.A., & Lerner, G.H. (2009). When are persons 'white'?: On some practical asymmetries of racial reference in talk-in-interaction. *Discourse & Society, 20*(5), 613–641.

Widdowson, H.G. (1994). The ownership of English. *TESOL Quarterly, 28*(2), 377–389.

Widdowson, H.G. (1997). EIL, ESL, EFL: Global issues and local interests. *World Englishes, 16*(1), 135–146.

Appendix. Notes on transcription

Transcription conventions (modified from Atkinson & Heritage, 1984):

[[ ]]	Simultaneous utterances – (beginning [[ ) and (end]])
[ ]	Overlapping utterances – (beginning [ ) and (end])
=	Contiguous utterances (or continuation of the same turn)
(0.4)	Represent the tenths of a second between utterances
(.)	Represents a micro-pause (1 tenth of a second or less)
:	Elongation (more colons demonstrate longer stretches of sound)
.	Fall in pitch at the end of an utterance
,	Slight rise in pitch at the end of an utterance
-	An abrupt stop in articulation
?	Rising in pitch at utterance end (not necessarily a question)
CAPTIAL	Loud/forte speech
__	Underline letters/words indicate accentuation
↑ ↓	Marked upstep/downstep in intonation
° °	Surrounds talk that is quieter
hhh	Exhalations
.hhh	Inhalations
he or ha	Laugh particle
(hhh)	Laughter within a word (can also represent audible aspirations)
> >	Surrounds talk that is spoken faster
< <	Surrounds talk that is spoken slower
(( ))	Analyst notes
( )	Approximations of what is heard
$ $	Surrounds 'smile' voice.

Index

Note: Page numbers in *italics* represent figures and illustrations
   Page numbers in **bold** represent tables

acculturation 72
Adil, Alev 33
aesthetics and ethics 11–12, 21
age as a factor influencing language choice by
   Japanese retirees 70
*Always On. Language in an Online and
   Mobile World* (book) 78
Arab Spring, the 31
Archaeology under Fire (book) 33
architectural history 33
'argot' (secret language) 89–90
Aristotle 11, 16, 73
autoethnography 22
awareness raising as the key to conflict
   prevention 13, 15

bias of visual recordings 31
Bitterfelder Weg, the 40n2
BOGOF (Buy-One-Get-One-Free) scam with
   domestic helpers 51
British experience of ICC 2–3
Broken Middle, The (book) 23

chain-posting 86–8, *87, 88*
challenges to English language hegemony 14
church shelters as accommodation for FDHs
   47–8
CMC (computer-mediated communication)
   6–7, 79–81, 92 *see also* study on the
   in-depth interview as a research tool
   for investigating online intercultural
   communication
collection of consciousness as research
   method 21

Common European Framework of Reference,
   the 11
community radio in India and social change 29
compartmentalisation of events, theory of 39
contemplation, phenomenon of 72–3
counter-memories and official historic
   discourse 28–9
creativity and the arts in interculturual
   language educaiton 13
cultural shock 72

decolonizing research methodologies 20
deductive approach to the study of social
   categories 96
developing a practice of intercultural ethics
   19–20
dialogue and self-knowledge 53
differences between German and Filipino
   postings on social media 85–8, *87, 88*
differences in language use online and face-to-
   face 90–1

Écriture automatique 40n2
EFL (English as a Foreign Language)
   see study on the relevance of ELF as
   an equitable social category in online
   intercultural communication
ELF (English as lingua franca) 6, 7, 71, 74, 89,
   96 *see also* study on the relevance of ELF
   as an equitable social category in online
   intercultural communication
EOKA B 36
equity as social justice 4, 75
equity through the spread of the Internet 78–9

ethics and language competence 71
ethics and Oral History 5, 28–30
European experience of ICC 3

Facebook 79–80, *84*, 85–7, *87*, 90
factors to consider when migrating 62; reasons
    for emigration 61, 75
FDHs (foreign domestic helpers) in Hong
    Kong 44–5, 57n4 *see also* study on
    exploitation of ethnic minority FDHs in
    Hong Kong
fear that use of social media will undermine
    the use of language 90–1
Filipino use of language in social media 85–8,
    87, 88, 91
Folman, Ari 33

German use of language in social media 85–8,
    87, 88, 91
Glenister Roberts, Kathleen 80
globalization 96

*Handbook of Critical Intercultural
    Communication, The* (book) 2
hermeneutic epistemology and the
    ethnographer 86
Hongladarom, Saraj 79, 92
humans as ethical beings 3–4
Huntington's clash of civilizations thesis 1

IALIC (International Association
    for Languages and Intercultural
    Communication) 2
ICC (intercultural communication) 1–4
ICOPROMO and INTERACT projects 14
identification process and cultural change 90, 91
identity in Cyprus 27–8
Imagined Communities (book) 33
importance of storytelling 45, 46
in-depth interview in intercultural research
    81–2 *see also* study on the in-depth
    inerview as a research tool for investigating
    online intercuturual communicaiton
indigenous peoples and research 19–20, 22
inductive approach to the study of social
    categories 96
institutional mode of OH narratives 39
intercultural awareness in a multilingual
    environment 88–9

intercultural discourses 45
International Association of Languages and
    Intercultural Communication 12
internet access and equity 78–9
intertextuality in interviews 32
interviews for OH history 35–9

Japanese retirees in Malaysia 6, 61 *see also*
    study on language choice by Japanese
    retirees in Malaysia

language: in CMC 6–7, 79–81; and
    communication and ICC 4, 6–7, 61–2;
    through intercultural social media 82–4,
    84, 87, 100–4
language and intercultural ethics 10–15
language proficiency by Japanese retirees in
    Malaysia *65,* **66**
Ledra Street (book) 33, 37
liquid modernity 16–17
Look East Policy, the 61

Malaysia as destination for migrant retirees 62–3
management ethics of profitabiltiy 12–13
Marcos, President Ferdinand 84
Mars Language, the 91, 92
MCA (membership categorization analysis)
    99–100
McLuhan, Marshall 30–1
Mediterranean Oral History Project, The 34
Mediterranean Voices: Oral History and
    Cultural Practice in Mediterranean Cities
    (2002–2005) 34
methodological approaches to CMC research
    80–1
methodological creativity and artistry in
    research 22, 23
migration by retirees 61, 62
mindfulness and consciousness in intercultural
    communication 14
MM2H (Malaysia My Second Home)
    programme, the 6, 61, 62–3 *see also* study
    on language choice by Japanese retirees in
    Malaysia
modes of OH narratives 39
moral exclusion and ontologisation 54–5

Nadjarian, Nora 33, 37–8, 39, 40
narrative therapy 46–7

New Media and Intercultural Communication
  (book) 79
Nicomachean Ethics (book) 11
non-integration of British retirees 72–3

OH (Oral History): and ethics 5, 28–31; and
  identity 32–3
ontologisation and ideologies of moral
  exclusion 54–5, 56

Parallel Trips (film) 34
participatory action research 21
personal memory and the politics of history 33–4
postmethod pedagogies 13–14, 16–17
poststructuralism and positions of neutrality 23
public discourses of Filipino domestic workers
  54–6

reactions by interviewees to a traumatic event
  38
reasons for migration by Japanese retirees 61, 75
refashioning of architectural history as
  political goal 33
*Research Methods in Human-Computer
  Interaction* (book) 80–1
research methods of ethical intercultural
  relationships 16–23, 104–5, 106
research on FDHs (foreign domestic helpers)
  5–6
research on marginalized groups 5–6
restorative methods for intercultural research
  21, 22

second naiveté 20, 21
SHARP project, the 27–8, 30
Silver Hair Programme 62
social capital 73
social categories in linguistics research 95–6
  see also study on the relevance of ELF
  as an equitable social category in online
  intercultural communication

social exchange theory and human self-interest
  71
storytelling 45, 46–7
study on exploitation of ethnic minority FDHs
  in Hong Kong 45, 47–56, 57n4
study on language choice by Japanese retirees
  in Malaysia **63**, 63–6, *65*, **66**, 68–71; in
  formal situations 66–7, **67**; in use of media
  67–8, **68**
study on the in-depth interview as a research
  tool for investigating online intercultural
  communication 80–5, 88–93; German and
  Filipino use of language in social media
  85–8, *87*, *88*, 91
study on the relevance of ELF as an equitable
  social category in online intercultural
  communication 96–9
study on the uses of OH (Oral history) in
  Cyprus 27–8, 31, 33, 34–41
symbolic competence 20

Tagalog 83–5
Taglish *84*, 85
Truth and Reconciliation process in South
  Africa 30

underpayment of FDHs in Hong Kong 49
Unemployed Writers Workshop, the 28
US assimilation of immigrants 1–2
use of the dominant language by bilingual or
  multilingual speakers 69

veiling of women 15
video recordings of research interviews 30–1
virtual language contact and affect on
  language development 90
'VisionBytes' 31

Waltzing with Bashir (book) 33
Western feminism and veiling 15
World Internet Project, the 31

For Product Safety Concerns and Information please contact our EU
representative GPSR@taylorandfrancis.com Taylor & Francis Verlag GmbH,
Kaufingerstraße 24, 80331 München, Germany

Batch number: 08153807

Printed by Printforce, the Netherlands